Factory
Chris van Uffelen
Design

BRAUN

CONTENTS

Sheltering the World's Gross Product

by Chris van Uffelen

At first glance, factories appear to be one of the most elemental construction tasks. At the same time, they are also examples of the most extreme type of architecture which closely approaches the notion of a pure enclosed space. Combine frame and shell, floor plate and roof, add building services, windows and doors, and the factory is finished. Assembly halls and warehouses don't require complex spatial relationships or sophisticated view juxtapositions. A closer examination, however,

reveals the complexity of these buildings. It is precisely this complete freedom of a simple closed space that makes these structures so interesting. Whereas "assembly line" factories offer bare functionality, architectural design often has to compete with industrial pre-fabricated buildings on a very small budget, being forced to create quality in detail using subtle means.

Of course, industrial architecture has much more to offer, answering not only to complex demands in terms of a smooth production process, but also anticipating future modifications and expansions. In addition, engineered services like heating and ventilation have to be joined with the often short-lived production equipment. When designing illumination, glare has to be minimized and the depth of the building calculated; air conditioning must not

interfere with modern IT technology. Similarly to office buildings, factories also have to offer infrastructure for informal inter-departmental meetings and spontaneous "on the go" exchanges. The logistics of the production process and infrastructure (delivery and dispatch) must be adjustable to changing processes and fulfill the strictest demands on time and energy savings. This is where the custom-designed factory can greatly outperform a pre-fabricated hall by considering the operator's specific needs during the design process.

The word factory comes from manufactory (from Lat. manus facere = manual production), which originally described quite the opposite of industrial production that characterizes factories. But the origins of the word point to one of the roots of the type building it denotes. Manufactories, also represented in this book, are based mainly on human labor, while factories are dependent on machines and energy sources. An early example of mass production based on manual labor was the medieval work shed, whose late Latin denomination fabrica makes up the root of countless words for factory (in German, Italian, Spanish, Turkish and other languages). Stones for construction of cathedrals were cut by stonemasons one by one, and masons' marks cut into these were used to calculate payment. Preparing stones in the winter was made possible only after the introduction of the work shed. In modernity, manufactories were built for goods where complex processes had to take place at one location, as in production of high-quality porcelain. Rarely were they as architecturally articulated as the Royal Saltworks built for Louis the XV by Claude-Nicolas Ledoux in Arc-et-Senans (1779). Although salt production belongs to heavy industry rather than to handiwork, the saltern is a representative sovereign architectural project instead of a functional building. Johann Heinrich Schüle's muslin factory in Augsburg (1770) copies the three-winged layout of a castle. As these buildings demonstrate, production halls have always been a calling card of their products.

///

The manufactory transformed itself into factory in the context of Industrialization taking place in England at the end of the 18th century. Creation of large production facilities staffed by unskilled workers was also facilitated on the continent by free enterprise brought about by the dissolution of guilds after the French Revolution. Water-powered looms were already in use in the textile industry in the 16th century. In 1786, Edmund Cartwright patented his steam-powered loom. The textile industry usually occupied multi-storied support-free buildings that stood near water; the steam

engines (James Watt, 1784) needed coal and therefore, railroad connections – in contrast to manufactories, factories are extremely dependent of their environment and infrastructure. In this sense, they continue along the tradition of mills, which use kinetic energy of water or wind and employ only a handful of workers. Starting around 1840, the buildings became primarily one-storied because of louder and heavier machines, and in Northern Europe they were given shed roofs to facilitate illumination of the interior. Joseph Paxton's 1851 Crystal Palace built for London's World Exhibition already offered a model of a hall that had the potential to be expanded nearly infinitely, and system buildings quickly conquered industrial architecture. Examples of iron frame buildings include the Menier chocolate factory in Noisiel-sur-Marne by Jules Saunier, featuring Beaux Arts masonry. Around the turn of the century, many industrial operations moved to the outskirts of large cities, where cheap labor was readily available. Around the same time, other factories were being built far from urban centers, erecting variations of Ebenezer Howard's garden cities, completely independent of existing structures (e.g. New Earswick for Joseph Rowntree from Parker & Unwin, 1901). The ideal industrial city found its successor in Tony Garnier's Cité Industrielle, which was designed before 1904 and published in 1917. Many classical modernist architects were interested in the factory as a contemporary place of production. While the AEG turbine factory, built by Peter Behrens in Berlin in 1909, still aimed to transform Karl Bernhard's functional three-joint arcade hall into a temple with massive outer walls, the shoe last factory built in Alfeld an der Leine by Walter Gropius in 1910–1915, already has a largely functional form. The outer construction represents new fabrication methods found inside, indicating that the product being manufactured here is

↑↑ | **Warehouses Amsterdam**: former storage facilities
↑ | **Peter Behrens**, 1924: Hoechst factory
↗ | **Martin Hammitzsch**, 1909: former cigarette-factory Yenidze in Dresden
↗↗ | **Walter Gropius**, 1915: factory in Saalfeld
→ | **Brinckman en van der Vlught**, 1926: Van Nelle factory in Rotterdam

more modern than that of the competitor. In the case of the Van Nelle factory in Rotterdam by Brinckman en van der Vlught (1926–1930), the production process can be "read" in the structural volume. The Coca-Cola Building in Los Angeles by Robert V. Derrah (1936) is even more dynamic. The Margarete Steiff factory exemplifies that it was possible to build even more functionally. Built by her nephew Richard Steiff in Giengen an der Brenz, it reduced all its walls to a bare iron frame in 1903, 1904 and 1908. At the head of the movement were the Futurists, who had a soft spot for speed and mechanics and for whom factory architecture was an ideal. In comparison to their designs, even the Highland Park Ford Plant (1910), with its Ford T as the precursor of production rationalization (Albert Kahn; Edward Gray), seems quite traditional. The only realized Futurist project is the FIAT plant in Lingoto (Turin) built by Giacomo Mattè Trucco in 1915–1923 which features a test track on the roof. Around this time and following Second World War, the extreme environmental pollution created by factories as well as the functional segregation of living space proposed by the International Congress of Modern Architecture pushed mass production further and further away from cities. Systems buildings dominated the entire architectural sector after the war, with exceptions like Félix Candellas Bacardi plant in Carretera with an expressive succession of arched shells (1970). Neutral, expandable buildings such as those created by Kahn, Fritz Haller (USM in Münsingen 1962–1964), Eero Saarinen and SOM dominated the scene. The Reliance Controls factory built by Team 4 (Richard Rogers, Su Brumwell, Norman and Wendy Foster) in 1966–1967 in Swindon is exemplary of the period. The frame is quickly erected in an economical fashion, and is completely flexible due to its modular, expandable structure surrounding a series of inner yards. The additional benefit of the architecture is found on the one hand in the details, like the ribbon window below the roof, and on the other in the elevated social standards, testified by inner yards, missing separators between production and administration and common entrances for workers and office employees.

//

The first large-scale dying out of factories came with the iron and steel crises of the 1980s. Old complexes were turned into museums or were converted into loft apartments or offices. The transition to a post-industrial society has been ushered in by globalization, and is still continuing to this day. At the same time, new modern factories for novel products and production processes are being built in the old industrial nations as well as in those still undergoing industrialization. Not only do these appear much cleaner from the outside, but they must often fulfill clean room standards inside. Now nothing stands in the way of the factory returning to within the city limits, for this is where its appearance again becomes a valuable part of the company's identity.

↑ | **Richard Steiff,** 1908: Steiff factory in Giengen an der Brenz
↗ | **osa – office for subversive architecture,** 2007: reuse of a factory as Greenland Street theater, London
↗↗ | **Grimshaw,** 1981: Vitra factory, Weil am Rhein. Corporate identity by famous architects
→ | **Alvaro Siza,** 1990: Vitra factory, Weil am Rhein. Zaha Hadids fire-station in the background

Heavy
Industries

Bob Gysin + Partner BGP

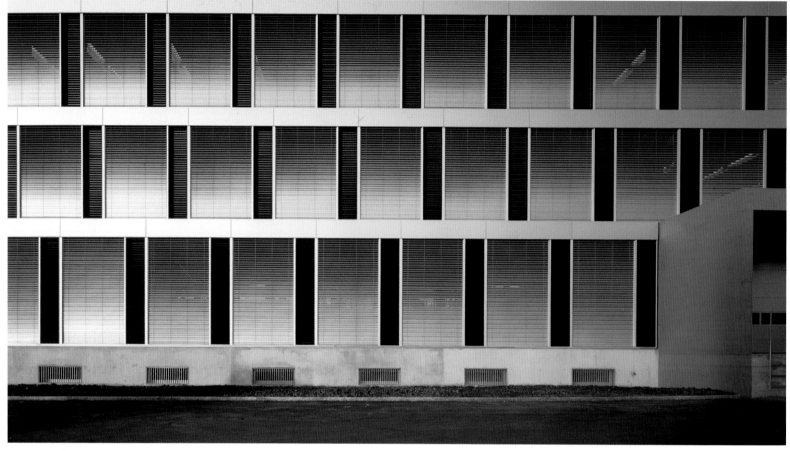

↑ | **Front façade,** detail

Longus Production Building
Hinwil

Together with a connecting body and the existing structure, the new five-story, 166 meter long building forms a clearly centralized complex to house research, production and office areas of the Belimo Automation AG. The delivery ramps and employee entrances, executed as colorful fair-faced concrete elements that lead to interior spaces with a variable layout, act as counterpoints to the building's glazed façade. The story-high glazing allows daylight to enter and simultaneously reveals views of the surrounding neighborhood, resulting a pleasant work atmosphere inside. The façade around the efficient frame consists of prefabricated elements which have been ordered in a staggered fashion from floor to floor. This gives the building a distinctive architectural appearance which only abstractly reflects the contents of the volume.

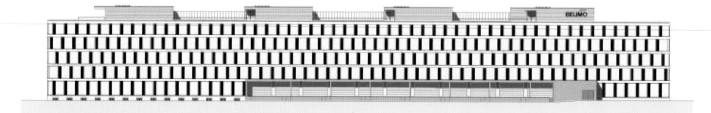

Address: Brunnenbachstrasse 1, 8340 Hinwil, Switzerland. **Client:** Belimo Automation AG. **Completion:** 2002. **Gross floor area:** 22,970 m². **Number of workplaces:** 300. **Main construction:** concrete frame with solid staircase core. **Roof:** flat. **Lighting:** daylight and fluorescent lamps. **Main materials:** prefabricated metal elements, glass, concrete. **Setting:** industrial.

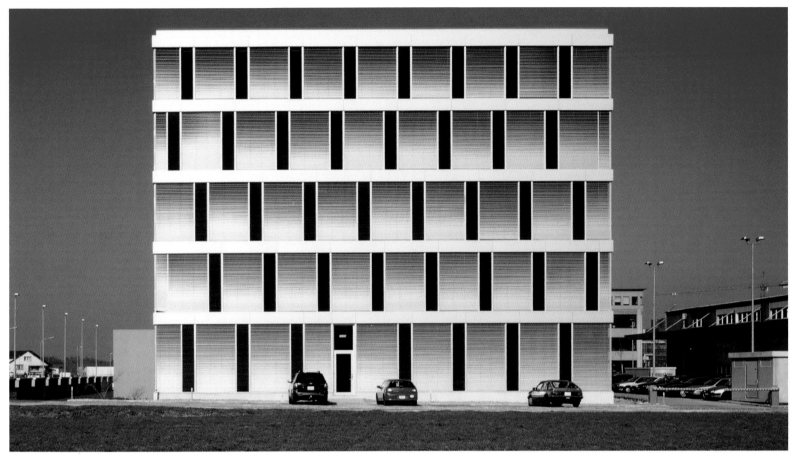

↑ | **Façade,** view upon narrow side of the building

↙ | **Plan,** south façade

↓ | **Front façade,** contrasting concrete elements

↑ | **Foyer,** clearly structured entrance area
← | **Staircase**

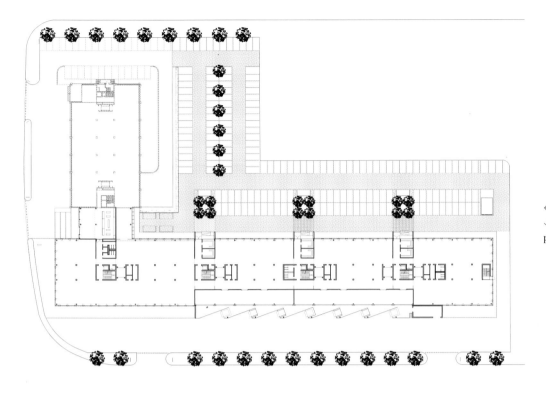

← | **Plan,** ground floor and situation
↓ | **Interior,** bright production area with
panorama windows

↑ | **Façade,** view of montage facility at night
→ | **Staircase,** view of the staircase of montage facility

Transparent Factory
Dresden

With its Transparent Factory, Volkswagen became the first manufacturer to realize a concept which combines the processes of classic industrial automobile production and craftsman-ship. In this factory luxury limousines are put together by hand. The Transparent Factory, in German "Gläserne Manufaktur", is a place of exchange and exposes the process of automobile production to the world outside. The building is not only the location of assembly, but also platform for TV productions, exhibitions and concerts.

Address: Lennéstraße 1, 01069 Dresden, Germany. **Client:** Volkswagen AG. **Completion:** 2001. **Gross floor area:** 81,800 m². **Number of workplaces:** 800. **Main construction:** steel composite girders and beams. **Roof:** flat. **Lighting:** daylight and fluorescent lamps. **Main materials:** glass, steel. **Setting:** urban.

↑ | Assembly area
← | Ground floor plan

← | **Visitors and event area,** view from fourth floor
↓ | **Visitors area and approach to park**

Prof. J. Reichardt
Architekten

↑ | **Perspective,** loading zone
↓ | **Night shot,** long range light effect

→ | **Detail,** offset façade
→→ | **Façade,** offset façade structure sheltering the loading zone

Logistics Center Blanco
Bruchsal

The Blanco company organizes the distribution of high-quality sinks from its location in Bruchsal. The newly erected logistics center is built in a modular fashion and may be expanded if needed. A wide steel frame with a support grid of 18 by 31.5 meters enables the highest possible flexibility. The overhanging office gallery shelters the loading area, and the element continues along the rest of the façade using repeating horizontal rows of glass and aluminum. This appearance of the building reflects the high design as well as precision quality demanded of the company's product. The building's massive reinforced concrete cores on the side of the gallery provide stability.

PROJECT FACTS

Address: John-Deere-Straße 32, 76646 Bruchsal, Germany. **Logistics:** Integral Consultance. **Technical engineers:** Ing. Büro Paulus. **Structural engineering:** Ing. Büro Fritz. **Engineers outer facilities:** Ing. Büro Turrek. **Client:** BLANCO ImmoLog GmbH + Co. KG. **Completion:** 2008. **Gross floor area:** 19,000 m². **Main construction:** steel truss with reinforced concrete core. **Main materials:** alu-cobond, textured glass. **Setting:** industrial.

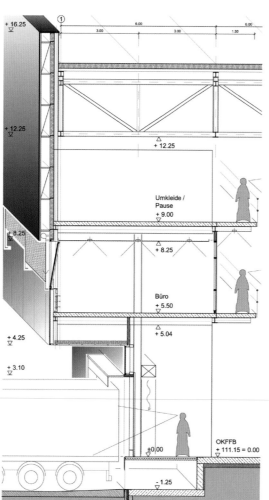

↑ | **Loading zone**
↙ | **Section**, façade

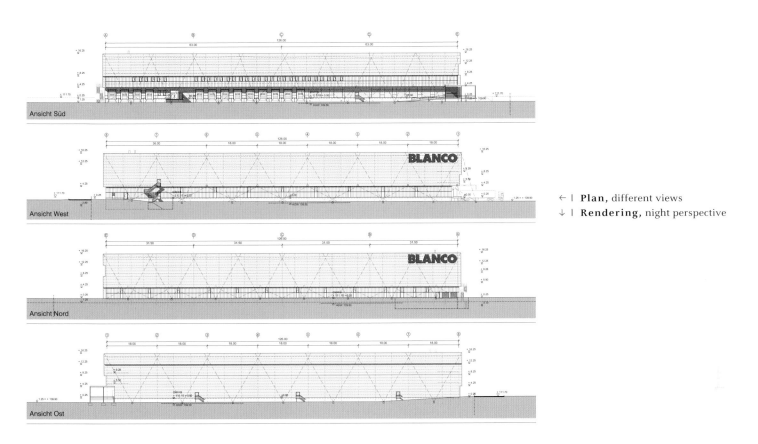

Ansicht Süd

Ansicht West

Ansicht Nord

Ansicht Ost

← | **Plan,** different views
↓ | **Rendering,** night perspective

↑ | **Exterior,** front view
→ | **Roof**

Schmitz Truck&Trailer Center
Senec

Sited in an as yet undeveloped area with only heavy transport infrastructure, the architect's intention was to announce the position of a building at this significant road junction. Having no desire to create another classic industrial boxed shed, they took inspiration from the landscape. In this winding and twisting terrain they enclosed an envelope around the required functions and also defined the external traffic flow. The defined functional areas are showroom, administration, driver interface, five repair bays and associated storage and parking lots.

PROJECT FACTS

Address: Dialničná cestá 16, 90301 Senec, Slovakia. **Client:** Central Europe Trailer. **Completion:** 2007. **Gross floor area:** 1,500 m². **Number of workplaces:** 20. **Main construction:** steel framework in combination with reinforced concrete parts. **Roof:** partly shed, partly flat. **Lighting:** through façade, roof skylights and artificial light. **Main materials:** aluminum sandwich panels, glass, exposed façade panels, plasterboard. **Setting:** rural.

↑ | **Exterior**
← | **Side façade**

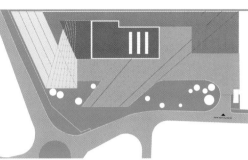

← | Showroom
↑ | Site plan
↓ | Ground floor plan

Søren Robert Lund
Architects

↑ | **Exterior**
→ | **Façade**

Printing Factory
Slagelse

The central motif of the printing house is the furrow, which is defined by the large build-ing volumes housing the printing and technical areas. The line of the furrow echoes the idea of the machine that folds the newspaper. The printing and ventilation halls are clad in folded zinc, which emphasizes the idea of folding around the furrow. To express this line further, the printing hall's façade creates a large inward-oriented shape, whereas the technical area creates a smaller outward-facing shape. The central element is flanked on each side by lower buildings, which contain administration, paper storage, packing area and cafeteria.

PROJECT FACTS

Address: Skovsøvej 27, 4200 Slagelse, Denmark. **Client:** Jydske Avistryk A/S. **Completion:** 1999.
Gross floor area: 4,800 m². **Main construction:** steel, concrete. **Main materials:** zinc, concrete, wood,
steel, plaster. **Setting:** rural.

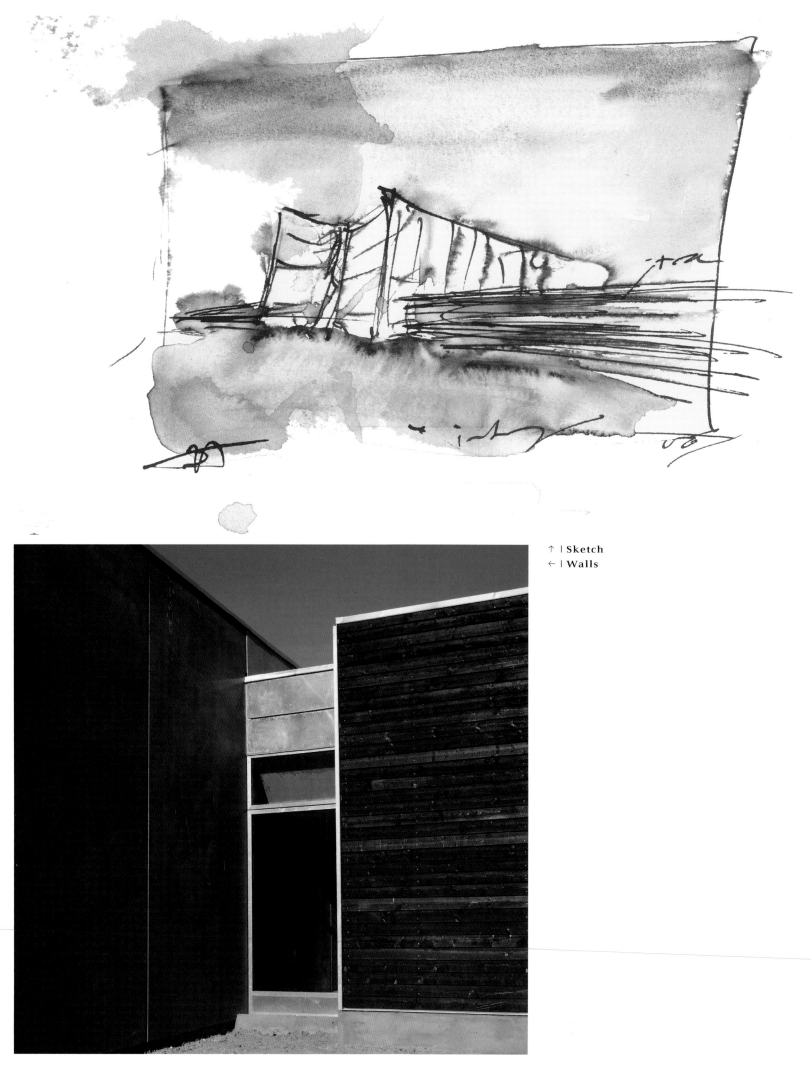

↑ | Sketch
← | Walls

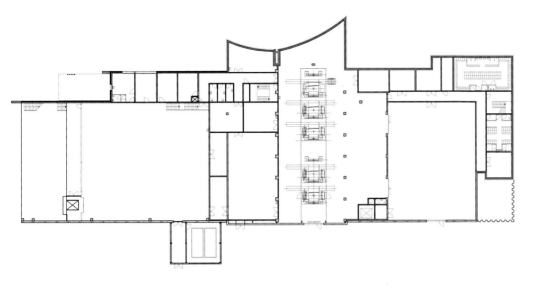

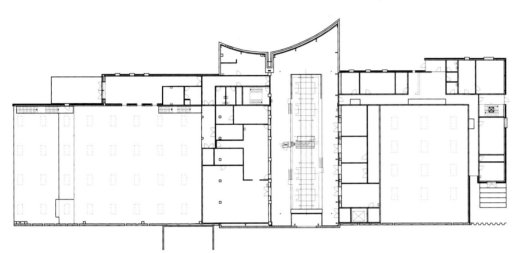

← | Sections
↓ | Entrance area

Prof. J. Reichardt
Architekten

↑ | **Entrance,** view by night

Modine Automotive

Wackersdorf

These automotive supplier assembly halls are the site of cooling element assembly. The design is based on a modular factory structure, which enables a high degree of versatility in respect to production processes, building expansion and alteration of building technology. The segmented façade structure allows retroactive addition of gates at any position. On the interior, the offices are suspended from the hall frame without any supports. Galleries with parquet floors connect individual offices, offering views of the entire production process to visitors and employees. Vertical lattice glazing brings continuous daylight to all areas of the hall.

Address: Arthur-B.-Modine-Straße 2, 92442 Wackersdorf, Germany. **Project manager:** C. Gottswinter.
Site manager: BePro U. Wieczorek. **Process planners:** IFA. **Technical planners:** Planungsgesellschaft Kar-
nasch GmbH. **Client:** Modine Montage GmbH. **Completion:** 2003. **Gross floor area:** 11,350 m². **Main construction:** steel framework. **Roof:** flat roof. **Lighting:** daylight and roof lights. **Main materials:** sandwiched
metal, textured glass. **Setting:** industrial.

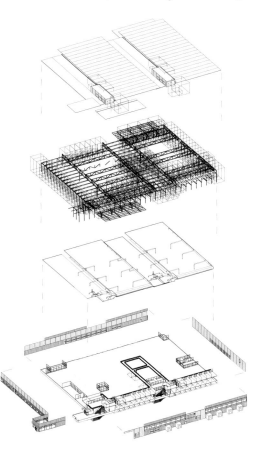

↑ | **Explosion**
↓ | **Loading zone,** view by night

↑ | **Administration,** offices suspended from
steel trusses

N Maeda Atelier /
Norisada Maeda

↑ | **Front elevation,** façade
→ | **Corridor,** interior view

Phiaro

Tochigi

Phiaro is a company that develops car design. To give the factory's separate rooms a strong relation to the red belt, the visitor passage has been wound around three separate boxes that serve as studios. With its alternating elevation it creates a new relation of the boxes to each other. Strong color schemes give each room its own identity and create a corporate identity linking the spaces to one another.

PROJECT FACTS

Address: Hagadai 113, Haga-cho, Haga-gun, Tochigi, Japan. **Other creative:** e-house archi collaboration. **Client:** Phiaro corporation Takeichiro Iwasaki. **Completion:** 2003. **Gross floor area:** 1,300 m². **Main construction:** reinforced concrete. **Roof:** flat. **Lighting:** fluorescent lamp. **Main materials:** reinforced concrete, galvalume. **Setting:** rural.

↑ | **Studio c5**
← | **Roof garden,** night view
↓ | **Sections**

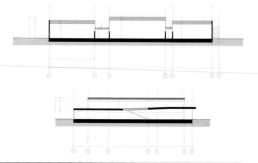

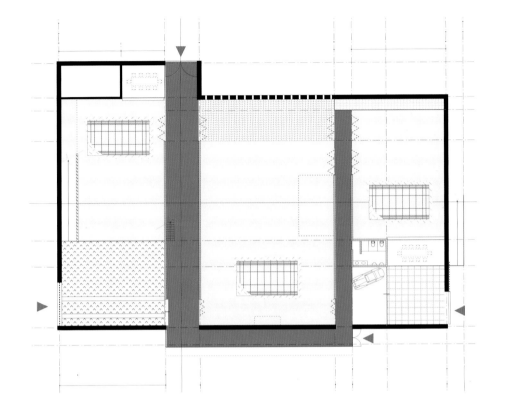

← | **First floor plan**
↓ | **Gallery**

Melkan Gursel &
Murat Tabanlioglu

↑ | **Inner courtyard,** outdoors recreational area
for the use of the employees
→ | **Corridor,** uninterrupted vast corridors benefit
natural daylight

Dogan Printing Center
Izmir

The strong horizontal emphasis in the architectural form expresses the function of the
printing center. The materials, mainly monochrome insulated metal panels, fair-faced
concrete blockwork and high-level horizontal glazing, without superfluous embellish-
ment, are similarly expressive of the building's purpose. The form with its somewhat
austere angular grey profile has a close affinity to those produced by the Bauhaus in the
late 1920s.

PROJECT FACTS

Address: Ege Cad. No. 36 Sarnıç 35410 Gazi Emir, Izmir, Turkey. **Client:** Hürriyet Gazetecilik ve Matbaacilik. **Completion:** 2006. **Gross floor area:** 17,000 m². **Number of workplaces:** 300. **Main construction:** steel and reinforced concrete. **Roof:** flat. **Lighting:** artificial in the print house, artificial and natural in the offices. **Main materials:** glass, insulated metal panels, steel. **Setting:** industrial.

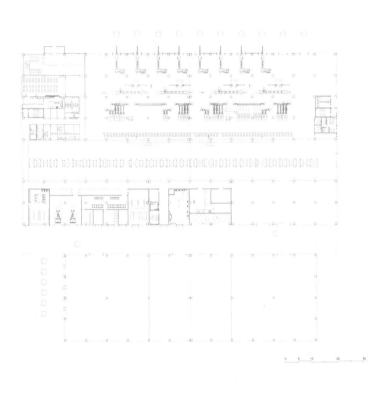

↑ | **Ground floor plan**

↑ | **Production hall,** simple geometry from the superimposition of a production flow diagram

↑ | **Front elevation**
→ | **Side elevation**

Age Developments
Malaga

The client's brief was to construct a large factory and warehouse with an attached administration and office area. As it was the first building in a new commercial subdivision it was important to create an easily recognizable landmark building. The development was oriented to allow 'road trains' easy access to the factory/warehouse from the main road. The office administration area was located on the corner of the site, allowing it to act as a beacon, giving high visibility and also creating an easily accessible street frontage to visitors. The natural irregularities of the site allowed the office to be at a level much higher than the warehouse resulting in passive surveillance of the factory floor.

PROJECT FACTS **Address:** 38 Harris road, Malaga, WA 6090, Australia. **Client:** Age Developments. **Completion:** 2005. **Gross floor area:** 7,111 m². **Main construction:** concrete dado panel, steel framework with trimdek wall cladding. **Roof:** raking on 3° pitch. **Lighting:** translucent roof panels, artificial. **Main materials:** concrete tilt panel, colorbond trimdek wall cladding, exposed steel framework. **Setting:** industrial.

↑ | **Entrance** with parking area

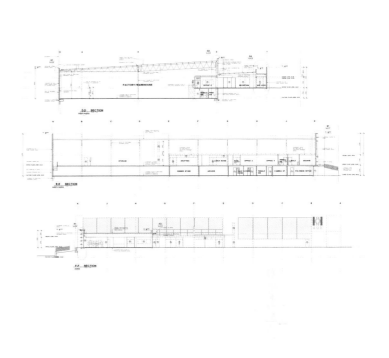

↑ | **Sections**

MDN Marco Visconti &
Partners, Maire Engineering

↑ | **Exterior view**
↗ | **Site**
→ | **Entrance**

Ferrari Production Hall

Maranello

The facility is an avant-garde building characterized by advanced design expressions in the industrial field. The external part of the building is dominated by greenery, which filters direct views, underlining the views of nature experienced through the glass façades. Attention has been given to environmental comfort and light values, transparency and visual contact with nature. The façade system was conceived through the analysis of exposure and solar radiation. A sun-shielding portico was employed on the southern front constructed using perforated aluminum elements. On the eastern side, three glasshouses have been integrated, incorporating vertically-operated curtain movement.

PROJECT FACTS **Address:** Maranello, Italy. **Client:** Ferrari. **Completion:** 2002. **Gross floor area:** 14,500 m². **Number of workplaces:** 300. **Main construction:** steel framework. **Roof:** flat with skylights. **Lighting:** natural lighting through façade and skylights. **Main materials:** glass, aluminum, steel, concrete. **Setting:** industrial.

↑ | **Conference room** with view into the production hall

← | **Side elevation** with canopy and entrance

← | Detail
↓ | Ground floor plan

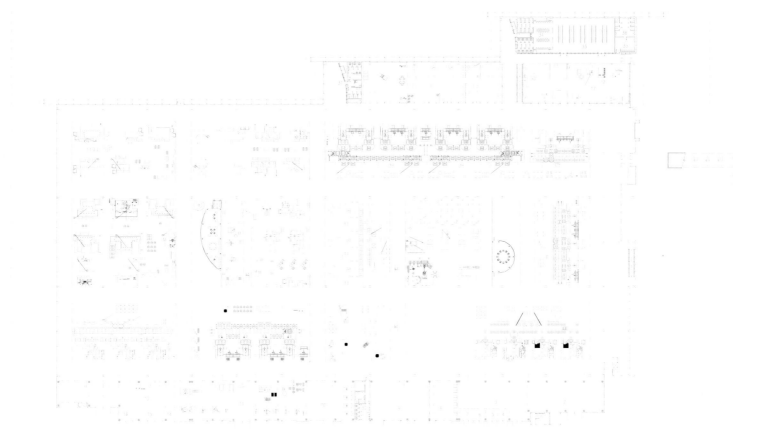

Laatio Architects /
Jari Kuorelahti

↑ | **Office building,** brick façade
→ | **Glass double façade**

Jot Automation Group Plc
Oulunsalo

The group's main office and factory are built in the immediate vicinity of the Oulunsalo Airport within the industrial estate that is being developed around the hub. In addition to production facilities and stores, training and personnel facilities are located on the ground floor of the production section. The personnel cafeteria and a kitchen were built in the office section of the building. In the production section, the first floor is reserved for planning and product development, while the first floor of the office section houses facilities for marketing and administration. The conference facilities and customer entertainment facilities are located above these.

PROJECT FACTS

Address: Automaatiotie 1, 90401 Oulunsalo, Finland. **Structural engineers**: Pekka Heikkilä. **Interior design**: Vesa Ervasti. **Artist**: Reijo Hukkanen. **Client**: Jot Automation Group Plc. **Completion**: 1999. **Gross floor area**: 13,898 m². **Number of workplaces**: 300–500. **Main construction**: steel framework and concrete elements. **Roof**: flat. **Lighting**: through façade, through roof and artificial. **Main materials**: brick, glass, stainless steel, concrete, steel. **Setting**: industrial.

↑ | **Exterior view** at night
← | **Lobby,** interior view of the stairs

← | **Interior view**, sculpture by Reijo Hukkanen
↓ | **Ground floor plan**

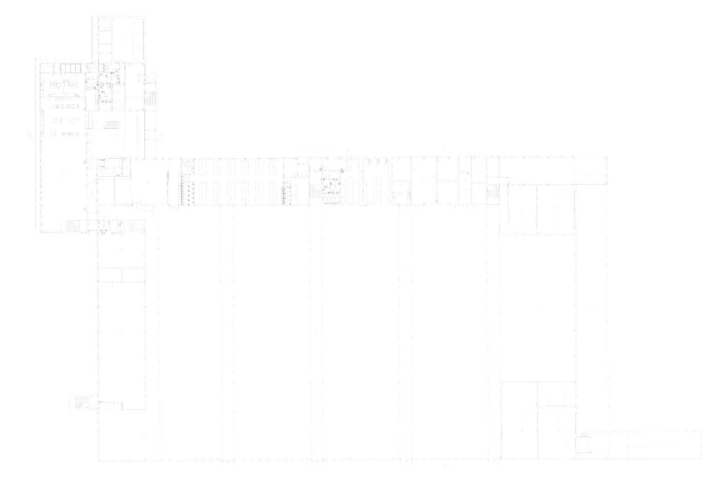

GATERMANN + SCHOSSIG

↑ | **Exterior view**
↗ | **Terrace,** test center
↗↗ | **Façade,** detail
→ | **Exterior view**

Capricorn Test Center
Meuspath

The automobile sports racing experimental and test center of the Capricorn company is located in direct vicinity to the author mile on the Nürburgring. The testing hall consists of a steel framework together with a BSH frame as a space-creating element. The functional two-story administrative wing houses an office area, sanitation facilities, changing rooms and relaxation rooms as well as the single-story workshop hall area, sectioned and successfully embedded into the natural topography. The color of the façades reflects the corporate identity of Capricorn and integrates the corporate identity ideas into the building's structure.

PROJECT FACTS

Address: Gottlieb-Daimler-Straße 17, 53520 Meuspath, Germany. **Client:** Capricorn Engineering GmbH.
Completion: 2003. **Gross floor area:** 1,044 m². **Number of workplaces:** 15. **Main construction:** steel
framework with BSH wooden framework. **Roof:** flat, aluminum panels roof. **Lighting:** inartificially
through façade and roof. **Main materials:** ferroconcrete, wood, glass. **Setting:** rural.

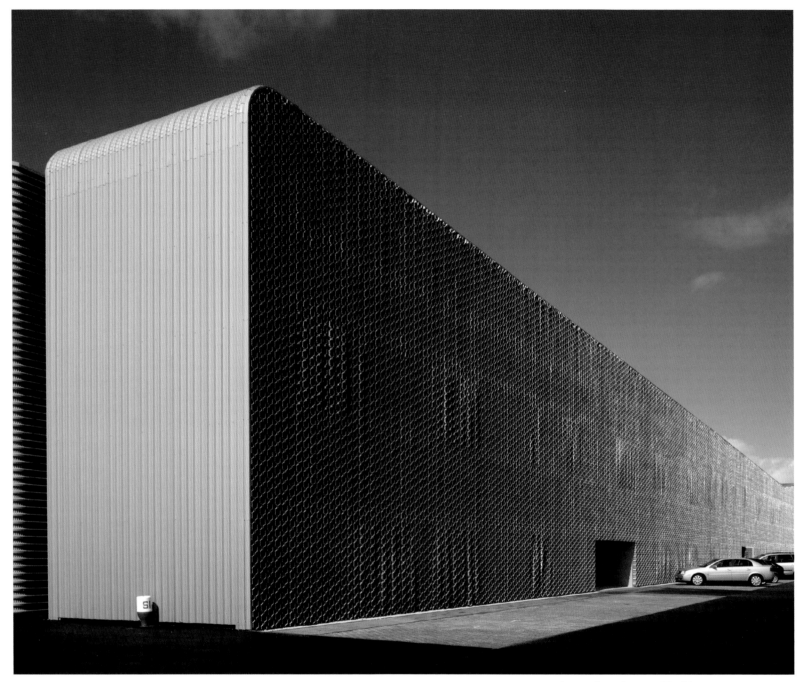

↑ | **East façade,** social building
→ | **Interior volume entrance**

Inapal Metal Industrial Unit
Palmela

The industrial unit is dedicated to the production of metal components for the automobile industry and is composed of two apparently autonomous volumes. One volume consists of two wings and a huge cantilever that combine raw material storage and different sections of production and delivery; while the other consists of two floors where the technical and social areas are arranged. The research is focused on the "skin" of the building. One unique surface material – trapezoidal metal cladding – furnishes and unifies all the project solutions: revetments sheets when a closed space is required; metal-sheet cut in slices and fixed like honey-comb when is essential to shade, illuminate or ventilate.

PROJECT FACTS

Address: Parque Industrial da Auto-Europa, Lote 2, Quinta do Anjo, 2950-678 Palmela, Portugal.
Client: Inapal Metal S.A. **Completion:** 2006. **Gross floor area:** 12,418 m². **Number of workplaces:** 30.
Main construction: steel framework (industrial plant) and concrete (social building). **Roof:** trapezoidal metal-cladding and plain metal-sheet. **Lighting:** fluorescent. **Main materials:** trapezoidal metal-cladding. **Setting:** industrial.

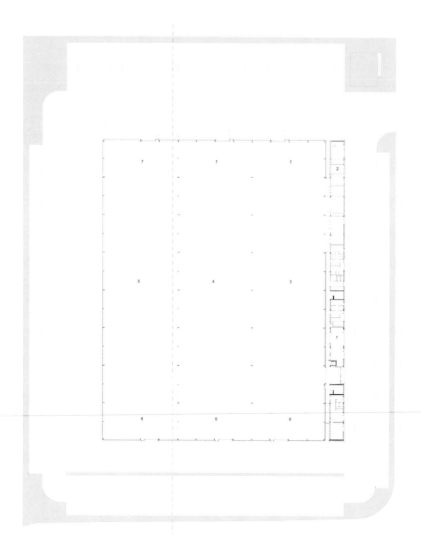

↑ | **Social building,** entrance lobby
← | **Industrial unit site plan**

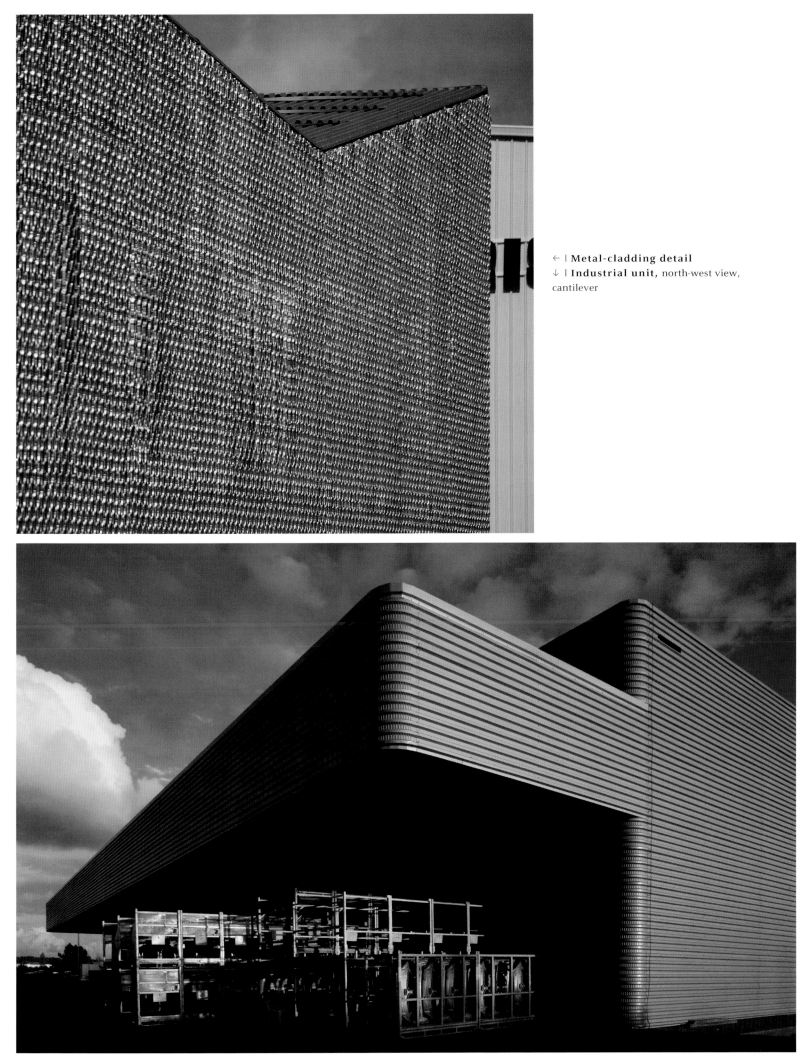

← | **Metal-cladding detail**
↓ | **Industrial unit,** north-west view, cantilever

Arkitektfirmaet
C. F. Møller

↑ | **North elevation** with turbine
→ | **R & D center,** side elevation

Vestas

Randers

Vestas wind turbine factory lies alongside the motorway and has been extended in several stages since its inauguration, most recently in 2002 with warehouse and administration facilities. The project included both external areas and interiors of the buildings. The architecture consequently finds expression on scales both large and small as a powerful unifying concept, providing the complex with a clear identity. The factory has been expanded in sync with the growing international success of Vestas. The complex shows that it is possible, despite changing demands, to maintain an overall architectural expression in a dynamic design process.

PROJECT FACTS
Address: Alsvej 21, 8940 Randers SV, Denmark. **Other creatives:** Rambøll, COWI, JPH, Amatech.
Client: Vestas Wind Systems A/S. **Completion:** 2008. **Gross floor area:** 35,000 m². **Main construction:**
concrete framework/steel framework. **Roof:** mixed. **Lighting:** roof/façade. **Main materials:** steel, concrete, glass panels, profiles. **Setting:** rural.

↑ | **Logistics center,** view from motorway
← | **Stairway,** interior view R & D complex

← | **Common areas,** negotiating ground level differences
↓ | **Site plan,** entire complex along motorway

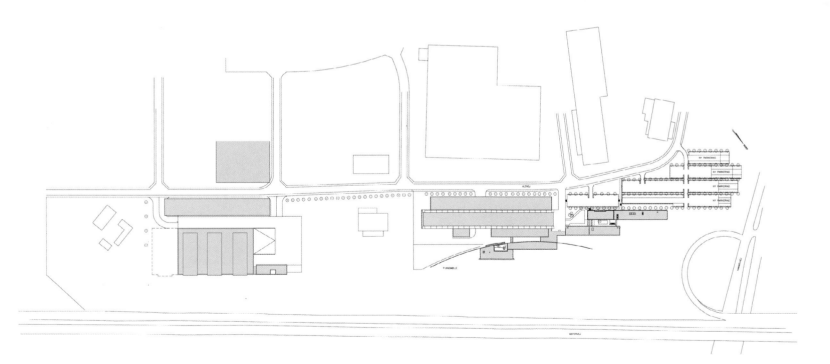

ATP Architects and
Engineers

↑ | **Shed roof** of production hall
→ | **Production hall** with façade band

Gerätewerk Matrei

Matrei am Brenner / Navis

Integrated design services were used for this building for a metal processing plant in
the Alps manufacturing heating and cooking equipment, sheet metalwork, etc. The concept is determined by the difficult topographic site characterized by an extreme hillside
situation. The façade was inspired by both the corporate culture of the client (a cooperative) and the idea of metalworking. A suspended metal structure unites building volumes
which are functionally very different (production, storage, R&D, administration) and reflects once again the cooperative ideal. Metal in its many potential treatments becomes
the image bearer of the building.

PROJECT FACTS

Address: Naviser Straße 1, 6143 Matrei a. Br./Navis, Austria. **Client:** Gerätewerk Matrei reg. Gen.m.b.H. **Completion:** 2005. **Gross floor area:** 11,300 m². **Number of workplaces:** 210. **Main construction:** steel columns. **Roof:** timber shed roof. **Lighting:** roof, continuous glazing in base, light deflecting slats. **Main materials:** alucobond façade strip, steel and aluminum elements, timber, concrete, glass, laminated panels. **Setting:** rural.

↑ | Administration building and
production hall
↙ | Sections

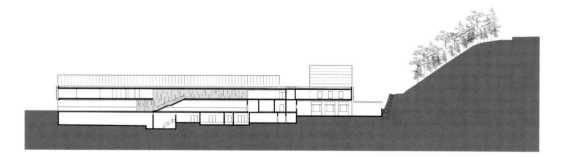

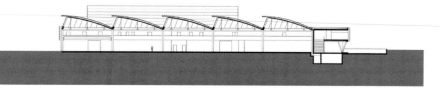

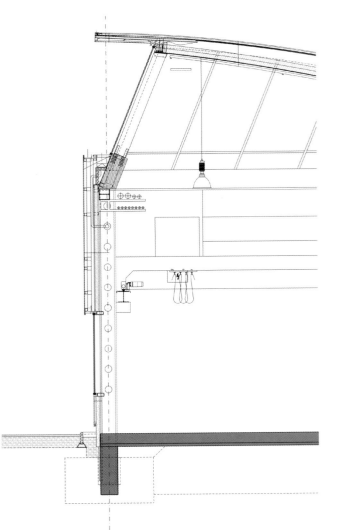

← | **Detail**, north façade
↓ | **Production hall** with light timber roof construction

↑ | **Street side elevation,** night view
↗ | **Interior view**
→ | **Ground floor plan**
→→| **Polycarbonate panels**

Gretsch-Unitas

Ditzingen

On a plot located at the entrance to the city of Ditzingen, a representative building was to be integrated into an existing structure from the 1950s in order to increase warehouse capacities. The erected building is a cube with a slender steel construction, filled out with translucent polycarbonate panels that transmit light inside as well as outside, simultaneously acting as highly efficient heat insulation. Beauty is thus united with use and function. A resilient, beaming and inviting building was thus created using clear lines, a simple form and a translucent façade.

PROJECT FACTS
Address: Johann-Maus-Straße 3, 71254 Ditzingen, Germany. **Client:** Gretsch-Unitas. **Completion:** 2006. **Gross floor area:** 2,152 m². **Main construction:** steel framework. **Main materials:** translucent polycarbonate panels, thin steel construction. **Setting:** industrial.

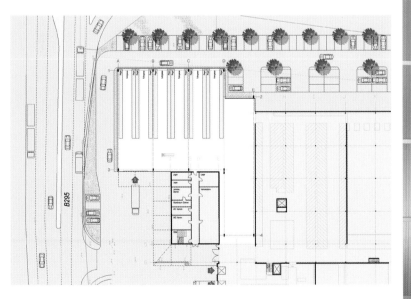

↑ | **Short front**
↗ | **Production hall and warehouse**
→ | **Goods delivery**

Stämpfli AG

Berne

The printing factory with its production hall, warehouse and offices consists of simply-built, cubist individual volumes that are connected to each other visually and organizationally, consolidating themselves into a larger form. For operational reasons, the production hall and warehouse are organized on one level. Delivery takes place from the side, and separate use of the production hall and the office building is also possible. The office building has a three-part organization, and all workplaces are oriented towards the open landscape. Production and warehouse are capable of being expanded to the south, and the office building can have stories added to it.

PROJECT FACTS **Address:** Wölflistrasse 1, 3006 Berne, Switzerland. **Client:** Stämpfli AG. **Completion:** 2003. **Gross floor area:** 13,800 m². **Number of workplaces:** 250. **Main construction:** supports and steel solid web girder. **Roof:** extensively greened platform roof. **Lighting:** through façade and selective through roof. **Main materials:** glass, dark wellband. **Setting:** industrial.

↑ | **Corridor,** view into production hall
← | **Production hall**

← | **Gangway** to parking area
↓ | **Second floor plan**
↓↓ | **Longitudinal section**

Amann Architekten /
Ingrid Amann Architektin

↑ | **Exterior,** view from south
→ | **Gallery**

Printing Factory

Munich

The idea of a uniform appearance dominates the design concept for the printing factory. The four façades are kept identical on principle. Functional necessities like canopies and overhead lights are not added elements, but are integral components of the building. The interior is defined by alternating single and three-story-high rooms, evenly-lit and connected by an open walkway. The transparent appearance of the façade opens the deep and shallow spatial layers and reacts separately to each light condition that emanates from inside the hall. The large overhead lights bring illumination into the recesses of the rooms.

PROJECT FACTS **Address:** Sigmund-Riefler-Bogen 9, 81829 Munich, Germany. **Client:** Riem GbR. **Completion:** 2000. **Gross floor area:** 800 m². **Main construction:** reinforced concrete. **Roof:** greened flat roof. **Lighting:** through façade and skylights. **Main materials:** figured glass, reinforced concrete. **Setting:** industrial.

↑ | **Interior**
← | **Exterior,** view from west

← | Stairway
↓ | Longitudinal section
↓↓ | Ground floor plan

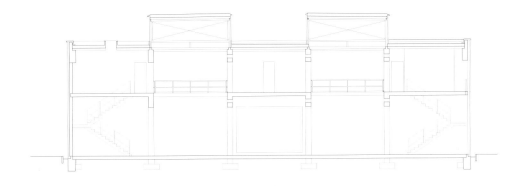

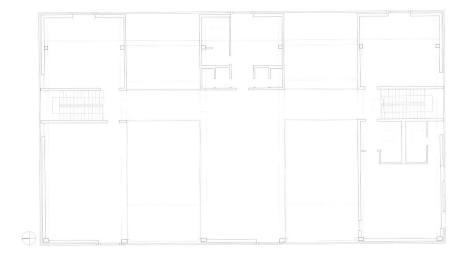

Dominique Perrault
architecture

↑ | **Exterior**

Aplix Factory

Le-Cellier-sur-Loire

The structure of the factory is the result of the juxtaposition of several 20 x 20 meter blocks, each 7.7 meters in height. In the initial proposal, the factory took the form of a long, regularly terraced rectangle. The main façade, which is over 300 meters long, faces onto the main RN23 road; windowless, it expresses the desire for internalization linked to the architectural project and to the confidentiality of the activity of production with the strict design of a thin, extended line from which a few treetops protrude. The visible material is slightly burnished metal sheeting. An idealized expression of agricultural buildings, it reflects the surrounding nature and allows the factory to gently blend into it.

PROJECT FACTS
Address: Les Relandières, 44850 Le-Cellier-sur-Loire, France. **Client:** Aplix S.A. **Completion:** 1999.
Gross floor area: 29,900 m². **Roof:** flat. **Lighting:** artificial. **Main materials:** metal. **Setting:** rural.

↑ | **Façade**, detail
↙ | **Elevation**

↑ | **Interior**
↓ | **Exterior**

↑ | **Front elevation**
→ | **Worm's-eye view,** angle elevation

VSM Factory

Hanover

The original VSM factory complex is executed in typical for Northern Germany turn-of-the-century red clinker façade, but its design has been obscured in the course of time with economically necessitated additions. A new production building on a more public plot acts as a prelude to the reclaiming of the factory as the company's business card. The profile sheeting façade not only picks up on the clinker's red color, but also appears as if it were manufactured using an VSM product due to the rough-textured additives: The façade projecting past the building volume appears to be an oversize sheet of sandpaper.

PROJECT FACTS Address: Sigmundstraße 17, 30061 Hanover, Germany. **Client:** VSM AG Hannover. **Completion:** 2002. **Main construction:** steel. **Roof:** EPDM roof membrane. **Main materials:** industrialized aluminum panel façade. **Setting:** urban.

MDN Marco Visconti &
Partners, Maire Engineering

↑ | **Transparency** as constituting design feature
↗ | **Site plan**
→ | **General view,** wing-shaped pavilion

Ferrari Company Restaurant

Maranello

The basics of the design consist in the juxtaposing of two volumes linked to concepts of aerodynamics as represented by the great hanging wing-shaped pavilion placed in a flight position supported by another staggered axis wing positioned vertically on the ground. Besides the aerodynamic design of the outside countenance a main goal for the architects was to create a recreational space enabling the experience of the surrounding nature.

PROJECT FACTS

Address: Maranello, Italy. **Client:** Ferrari spa. **Completion:** 2008. **Gross floor area:** 4,500 m². **Main construction:** steel and concrete. **Lighting:** natural lighting. **Main materials:** glass, aluminum, concrete. **Setting:** industrial.

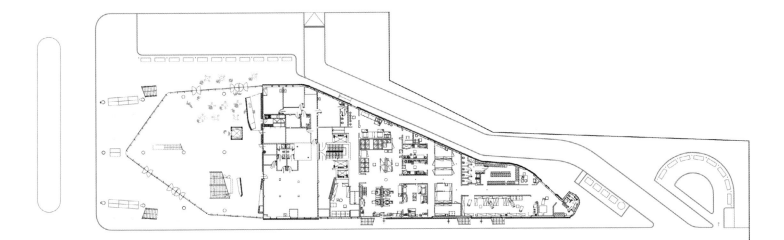

0 2 5 10 20 m

Gerken
Architekten + Ingenieure

↑ | **Exterior**
↗ | **Office area**
→ | **Assembly hall**

ESTA
Senden

The plot for the new assembly center was leveled by a team of architects and contractors. The building should reflect the ESTA company's innovative approach to work. It should be communicative and open, interlock administration, production and assembly and be heated and cooled completely with sustainable energy. The utilization concept envisions an encircling gallery of reinforced concert on the ground level that enables views into the assembly hall and simultaneously serves as an exhibition space. The central atrium stretches along the four administrative stories and is the company's communications center.

PROJECT FACTS

Address: Gotenstraße 2–4, 89250 Senden, Germany. **Planning partner:** Dirk Henning Braun. **Client:** Dr. Peter Kulitz. **Completion:** 2007. **Gross floor area:** 3,800 m². **Number of workplaces:** 100. **Main construction:** steel frame with reinforced concrete ceilings (fair-faced concrete). **Roof:** flat. **Lighting:** artifical, atrium. **Main materials:** glass, steel, concrete. **Setting:** industrial.

↑ | **Exterior** at night
← | **Stairway**, office area

↖ | Second floor plan
↙ | Section
↓ | Assembly hall

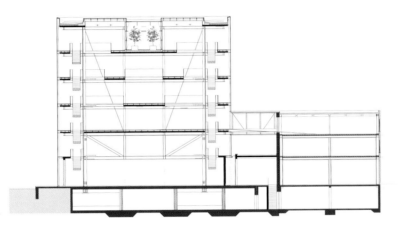

↑ | **Main entrance**, view of main entrance to integration center.

MAN Assembly Plant
Niepolomice

Heavy-duty trucks destined for the Central and Eastern European markets undergo final assembly at this plant. The factory premises are divided in a modular fashion into supply, assembly, logistics and accessory manufacture functional zones in accordance to the production flow. This makes it possible for all functional elements to be expanded individually in the future. The central factory gate is executed using dark gray brick and services all delivery, employee and customer currents. Assembly takes place in a compact, equally expandable hall. The paint shop and auto finish areas are added to the side as independent units. Material choice and details together project an image of precision and accuracy as well as genuineness and sturdiness.

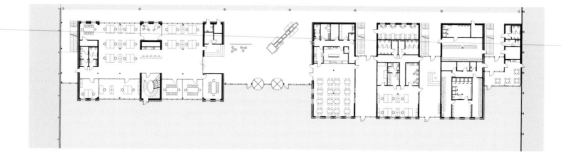

PROJECT FACTS
Address: MAN Trucks Sp. z o.o., ul. Rudolfa Diesla 1, 32-005 Niepolomice, Poland. **Partners in charge:** Pieter Frans den Haan, Christof Nellehsen. **Client:** MAN Nutzfahrzeuge AG. **Completion:** 2007. **Gross floor area:** 80,000 m². **Main construction:** steel framework. **Roof:** flat. **Lighting:** daylight through roof and façade, roof lights. **Main materials:** metal, glass, clinker. **Setting:** rural.

↑ | **View of main gate**
↙ | **Ground floor plan,** integration center

↓ | **Main entrance,** interior view

↑ | **Interior of integration center,** openness
and transparency as key concepts
← | **Staircase,** view of staircase in the integration
center

← | **Stairway in the integration center,** the dark grey bricks represent the company value "trustiness"
↓ | **Main entrance** at night

↑ | Circulation boulevard
↗ | Principal lakeside façade
→ | Façade backside

McLaren Technology Centre
Woking

The McLaren Group's new headquarters building, developed in part with the hi-tech company's own technology, is roughly semi-circular in plan and is completed by a formal lake which is an integral part of its cooling system. The principal lakeside façade is a continuous curved glass wall that looks out across the landscape and is shaded by a cantilevered roof. Internally, the building is organized around double-height linear streets, which form circulation routes and articulate fingers of flexible accommodation. These house production and storage areas on the lower levels, with top-lit design studios, offices and meeting rooms above.

High-
tech

↑ | **Die-casting hall,** north-west view

Alpla
Hard-Fussach

The building is arranged around a yard that is closed off on three sides, and through which visitors approach the five meter high entrance hall. The hall has a refined appearance thanks to its fair-faced concrete floor, wood-clad elevator center and a freestanding staircase in the middle of the room. The generous glass façade allows plenty of light to reach the interior. The volume is closed off with a flat roof. The glaziery docks directly onto the administrative building. The production hall, even with the ground, has a shed roof which provides an intense natural illumination. The façade consists of a sandwich element, in front of which a translucent polyester wave is suspended. The shipping area with out-facing docking stations is situated in the southern area of the glaziery. The fully automatic high bay warehouse delimits the space to the south.

PROJECT FACTS

Address: Lustenauerstraße 51, 6971 Hard-Fussach, Austria. **Client:** Alpla Werke – Alwin Lehner GmbH+Co KG. **Completion:** 2001. **Gross floor area:** 30,340 m². **Main construction:** reinforced concrete, wood brackets. **Roof:** flat. **Lighting:** light domes on the roof, partially continuous window rows on the façade. **Main materials:** covered sandwich panels, phenol resin panels, glass, polyester, reinforced concrete, birch wood. **Setting:** rural.

↑ | **Administration**
↙ | **Panorama**

↓ | **Administration,** reception area

↑ | High-rise warehouse
← | Trilateral enclosed courtyard

← | **Paint shop**
↓ | **Section**
↓↓ | **Elevation**, west

Valode et Pistre
architectes

↑ | **Aerial view**

L'Oreal Factory

Aulnay-sous-Bois

A flower blooms in Aulnay between suburban housing and a complex of industrial buildings. It spreads the three white "petals" of its corolla in graceful undulation around a green center. Each petal corresponds to a production unit and is a space free of interfering structures which nonetheless avoids uniformity. The three zones are independent of each other; suspended at mid-height above them, is an overhead walkway that also encompasses the interior garden. At Aulnay-sous-Bois, the L'Oreal factory is a manifest resolution of functional, formal and structural constraints: its architecture uses geometry to give poetic expression to the workplace.

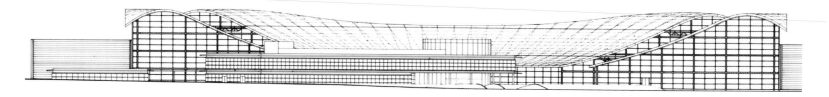

Address: La Barbière, Aulnay-sous-Bois, France. **Client:** L'Oreal. **Completion:** 1992. **Gross floor area:** 33,000 m². **Lighting:** through façade. **Setting:** suburban.

↑ | Interior view
↙ | Elevation

↑ | Roof
↓ | Courtyard

↑ I **View of entrance,** animated green lights guide visitors inside
↗ I **Façade,** view of dark colored front façade
→ I **Foyer,** dark colors contrasted by white furniture and green roof lights

Pinta Acoustic

Maisach

The company's new headquarters are based on a concept that is both minimalist and radical, following the customer's credo and corporate identity on the exterior as well as on the interior. The outer appearance is dominated by futuristic black cubes. A stainless steel-clad ramp with dynamic green light elements leads inside the building. The entrance hall is colored deep black like the façade, and features light grey seating and green and white light elements that lighten up the color scheme. The work areas, in contrast, are painted a cool white and interrupted by colorful accents. The architects used the customer's own products to decorate the interior, transforming the entire building into a showroom.

PROJECT FACTS

Address: Otto-Hahn-Straße 7, 82216 Maisach, Germany. **Client:** Pinta Acoustic GmbH. **Completion:** 2008. **Gross floor area:** 5,072 m². **Number of workplaces:** 100. **Main construction:** steel frame construction and reinforced concrete. **Roof:** flat. **Lighting:** roof lights and daylight. **Main materials:** concrete, aluminum, glass, linoleum, stainless steel. **Setting:** industrial.

↑ | **Cafeteria,** white and grey interiors are created by colorful chairs
← | **Plan**

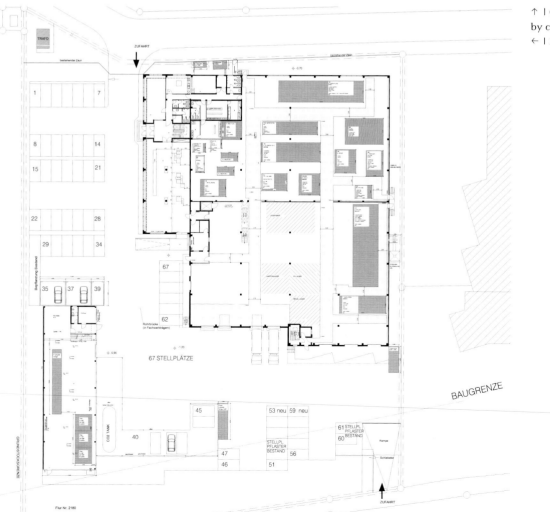

← | **Main staircase,** applied acoustic elements in light installations
↓ | **Head office,** view of conference area

↑ | **Façade,** view of the east façade of the building
↗ | **North façade,** the reflecting glazings of the
first floor create the impression of a floating edifice
→ | **North façade,** view by night.

Schiebel Group
Vienna

The building of the internationally active aviation industry supplier is organized into two areas: the office tract and the development and production area. The individual building sections are readily recognized due to the different façade materials used for each. The reflective glass façade on the ground floor creates an illusion of extending the surrounding landscape. This makes the office wing with a matte black basalt façade appear to float above ground. The production wing includes a 2,000 square meter production hall where in addition to manufacture and assembly, helicopter parts undergo development and maintenance.

Address: Viktor-Lang-Straße 30, 2700 Vienna Neustadt, Austria. **Structural engineers:** Büro D.I. Gritsch. **Client:** Schiebel Elektronische Geräte GmbH. **Completion:** 2006. **Gross floor area:** 4,955 m². **Main construction:** prefabricated basalt concrete. **Roof:** flat. **Lighting:** daylight through façade and roof, roof lights. **Main materials:** basalt concrete, aluminum, structural glazings. **Setting:** rural.

↑ | **Foyer,** the wing-shaped desk refers to the
company's industrial sector
← | **Ground floor plan and elevations**

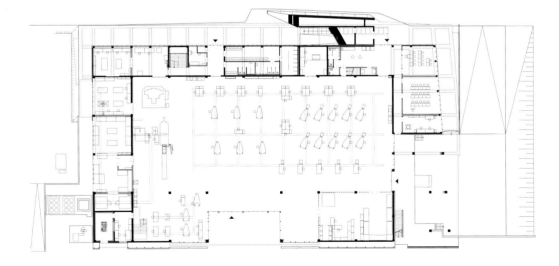

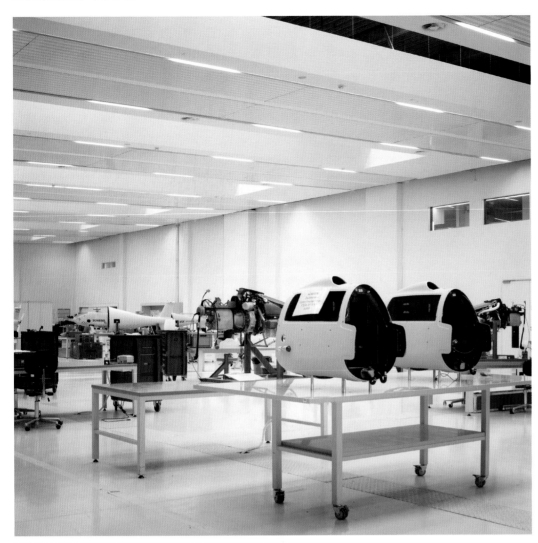

← | **Production area**
↓ | **Interior,** bright and noble designed spaces for the employees

pfeifer roser kuhn
architekten

↑ | **Main entrance**

Faller Pharma Service Center
Binzen

Building form and zoning connect functional and architectural elements into a simple ecological single concept using the principle of a Black Forest house, with a heating source at the center. The massive concrete construction with a non-insulated floor plate regulates the amount of heat, storing it and cooling the space. This enables the climate to be stabilized with minimal energy expenditure. All outer walls are built as passive air collectors – a construction of simple profile glazing, which stands in front of the massive walls with only an air gap, but without further insulation. The green-glimmering envelope transports the image of clean, pharmacologically applicable production processes as the outer image, becoming an expression of the company philosophy.

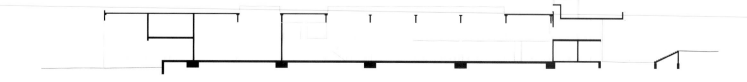

PROJECT FACTS **Address:** Meitner Ring 6, 79589 Binzen, Germany. **Cybernetics:** Delzer Kybernetik. **Building services:** ratio energie GmbH. **Statics:** Mohnke Bauingenieure. **Client:** August Faller KG. **Completion:** 2003. **Gross floor area:** 8,875 m². **Main construction:** reinforced concrete, frame construction and solid building. **Roof:** flat. **Lighting:** natural through roof and façade. **Main materials:** figured glass, wood, concrete. **Setting:** industrial.

↑ | **Exterior,** north-west elevation   ↓ | **Exterior,** north-east elevation

↙ | **Section**

↑ | **Open space office,** view to production hall
← | **Production hall**

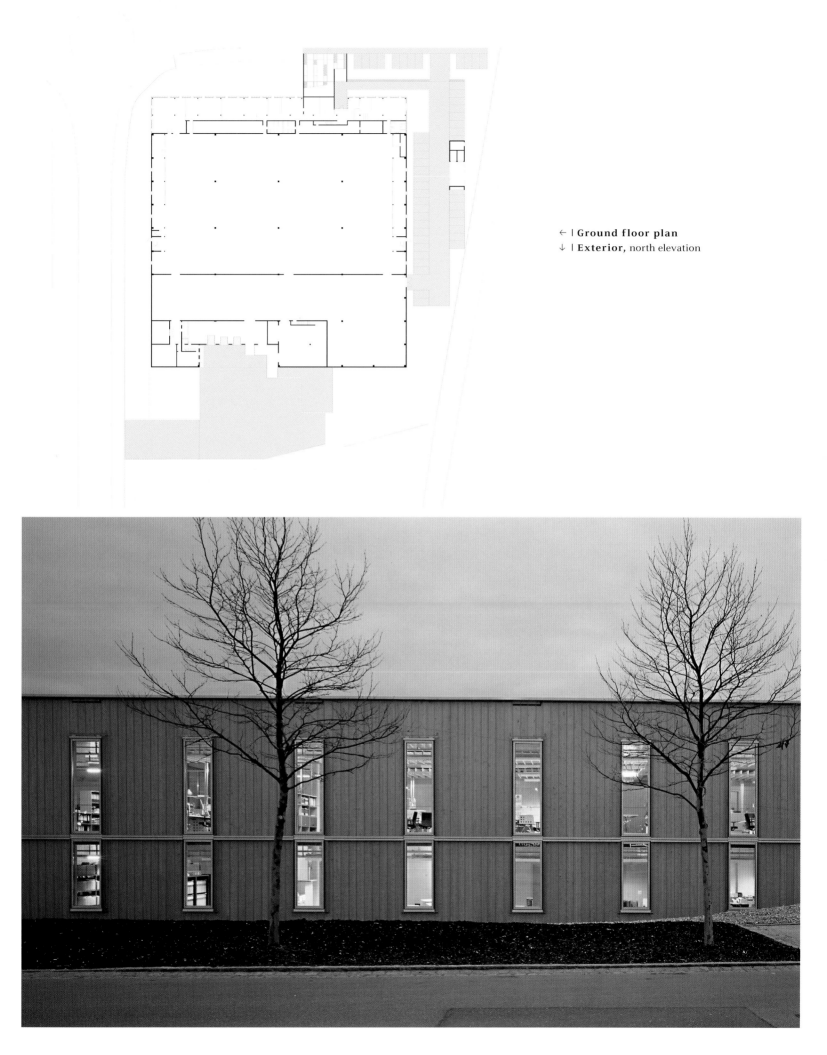

← | **Ground floor plan**
↓ | **Exterior,** north elevation

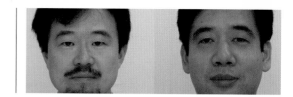

↑ | Exterior
↗ | Conveyor space
→ | Main entrance

Hogy Medical Tsukuba Kit Plant
Ushiku

Hogy Medical Tsukuba plant consists of the kit plant, an adjacent sterilization center and a distribution center. Here, medical equipment for surgery such as scalpels or clamps is assorted into pre-packaged kit. The clean rooms are located on the second, third and fourth floors. They are surrounded by a perimeter corridor and an air-tight curtain wall to prevent entrance of foreign objects, such as insects. The white translucent glass in the exterior curtain wall corresponds to the hygienic image of Hogy Medical as a medical equipment company. Natural daylight is introduced to the clean rooms through this curtain wall to secure amenity for the plant workers.

PROJECT FACTS
Address: Okuhara 1650-30, Ushiku, Ibaraki, Japan. **Client:** Hogy Medical Co., Ltd. **Completion:** 2002.
Gross floor area: 38,003 m². **Main construction:** steel framework. **Roof:** flat. **Lighting:** natural daylight.
Main materials: aluminum curtain wall, laminated film for clean room. **Setting:** rural.

↑ | **Assembly hall**
← | **Entrance hall**

← | Interior view
↓ | Bird's-eye view

↑ | **Administrative block,** the company's
outward face, in front of the production buildings

T&O Stelectric
Randers

Alongside the motorways lie all too many examples of mediocre buildings – despite the fact that they are seen every day by thousands of people. The T&O building beside the A 45 north of Randers turns over a new leaf: transforming motorway driving into an architectural experience. The building is created to be seen from the motorway and is aware of the obligations imposed by such a high degree of public attention. It is integrated into the motorway landscape as a two-story volume on the motorway side, with the more mundane production building behind. The proportions and details of the façade building, especially around the gables, make it a beautiful sight even to those just driving by.

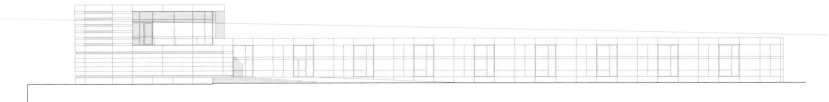

Address: Langelandsvej 6, 8900 Randers, Denmark. **Client:** T&O Stelectric A/S. **Completion:** 2005.
Gross floor area: 3,900 m². **Number of workplaces:** 130. **Main construction:** pillar-floor system (administration), supporting façade, tts-roofer (production hall). **Roof:** flat. **Lighting:** large transparent glass
façades. **Main materials:** electroplated steel plates, concrete elements with black stones, concrete
walls, staircases in high concrete. **Setting:** industrial.

↑ | **Exterior view**
↙ | **Elevation,** east façade

↓ | **East façade,** integrated into the motorway
landscape

↑ | **Stairway**
← | **The core of the building,** printer room,
toilets, kitchens, etc.

← | **Interior view,** glass façades provide daylight to the whole building
↓ | **Plans,** ground floor plan, first floor plan and section

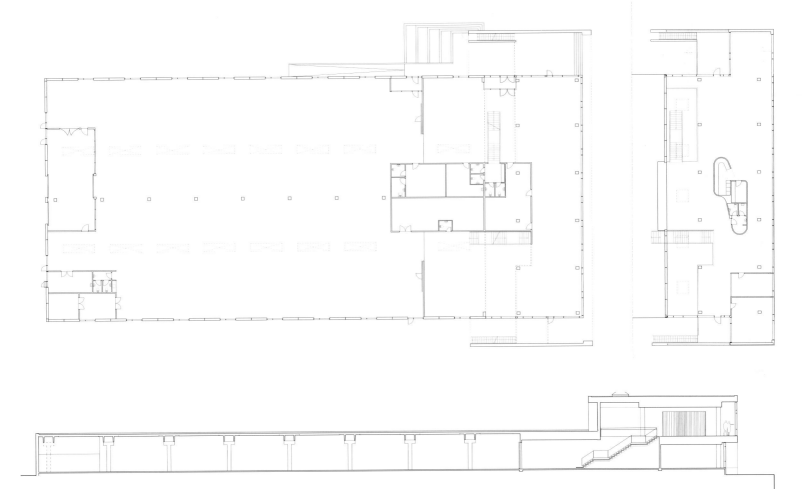

↑ | **Street side elevation,** façade facing the street

Steigereiland IJburg
Amsterdam

The building is an assembly workshop with offices for a company that develops hydraulic legs. The building will be located on the edge of IJburg in Amsterdam, bordering the water. The buildings' rectangular floor plan has been determined by the shape of the plot. The entry faces the street, and is marked by an exiting "cut" in the façade. This cut continues on the first floor, whereas the top floors have a closed façade with a skylight in the roof. The façade that faces the water is open, offering a view across the water. The only materials used for the exterior are Cor-ten steel, polycarbonate and glass; these materials create an industrial look that matches the companies character.

Address: Pedro de Medinalaan 13–31, Amsterdam, The Netherlands. **Client:** Steiger D. **Completion:** 2009. **Gross floor area:** 3,300 m². **Main construction:** prefab concrete. **Roof:** flat. **Lighting:** through façade, through roof. **Main materials:** Cor-ten steel, polycarbonate, glass, concrete. **Setting:** urban.

↑ | **Façade,** facing the water
↙ | **Façades**

↑ | **Façade,** facing the street
↓ | **Site,** bird's-eye view

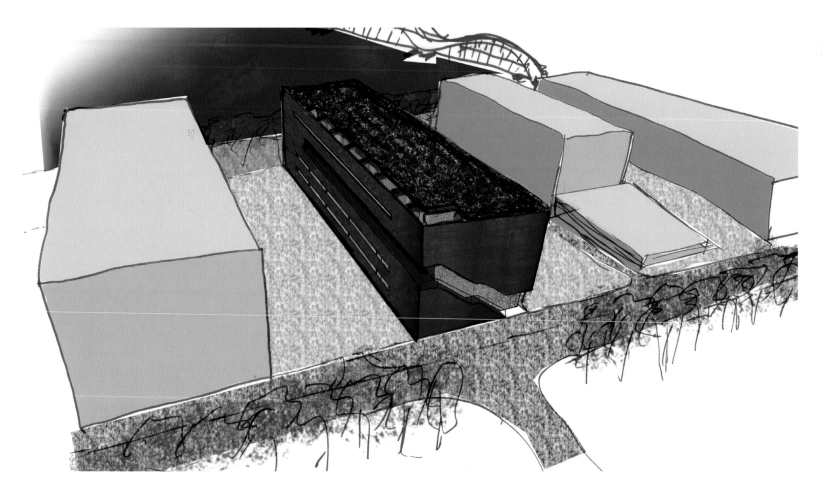

↑ | **West elevation**

Laser Machine Tool Factory

Ditzingen

Barkow Leibinger's first major project, a factory extension on a 40-hectare parcel, has been in planning since 1996. The project cultivates the landscape using the agricultural field structure as an organizing system for ordering the programmatic "parcels" of the new building. An axis connects existing and new factories, enabling pedestrian and fork-lift traffic. Industrial buildings are never finished, and theoretically, this one can infinitely expand into the fields along the motorway. The first two building phases are complete. Further additions will be made, constructing a carpet system of production halls of varying size and office spaces as new programs are created and available plots of land are developed.

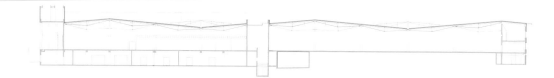

Address: Johann-Maus-Straße 2, 71254 Ditzingen, Germany. **Client:** TRUMPF GmbH + Co. KG.
Completion: 1998/2000. **Gross floor area:** 21,300 m². **Main construction:** reinforced concrete columns,
steel framework. **Roof:** steel trusses. **Lighting:** strip windows, diamond-shaped openings in the
roof, artificial light rows. **Main materials:** aluminum, concrete, steel, magnesite screed, natural stone.
Setting: industrial.

↑ | Lobby
↙ | Section

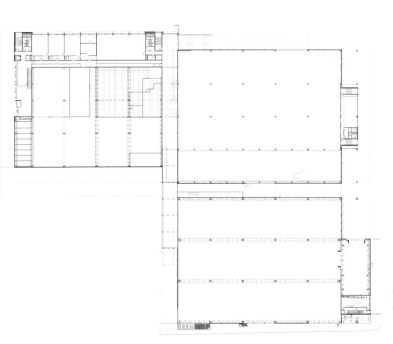

↑ | Ground floor plan
↓ | Production hall

Walter Nägeli, James
Stirling, Michael Wilford

↑ | **Administration building,** backside
→ | **Administration building and informa-
tion systems,** detail

Production Center Pfieffewiesen
Melsungen

The building of this production center is comparable to the laying down of a new town. Along the main axes, modern building typologies and lines for their development are laid down. This enables independent growth of single areas of the complex facility without risking losing its architectural character. The pedestrians who distribute out of the central parking garage into the buildings are connected with all parts of the facility like the delivery route, automatic goods transport system or the energy channels without disturbing intersections. The efficient production building is organized vertically in order to be able to be connected to communication routes without crossing them.

PROJECT FACTS
Address: Werk Pfieffewiesen der B. Braun AG., 34209 Melsungen, Germany. **Client:** B. Braun AG.
Completion: 1993. **Gross floor area:** 120,000 m². **Number of workplaces:** 800. **Main construction:**
reinforced concrete. **Roof:** vaulted roof. **Lighting:** through façade. **Main materials:** concrete, glass,
blue brick, aluminum, wood. **Setting:** rural.

↑ | **Administration building**
← | **Detail,** goods distribution center

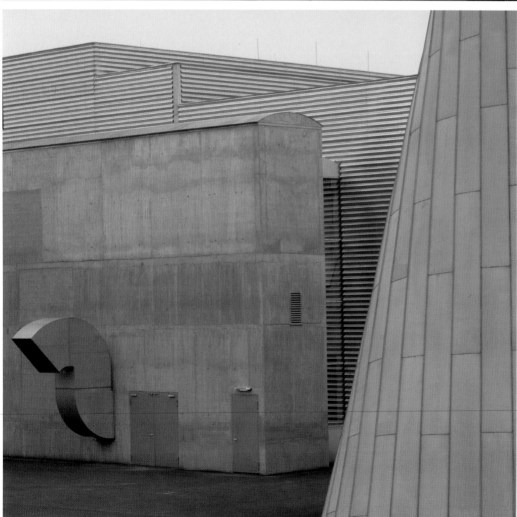

← | **Detail,** pedestrian walkway
↓ | **Site plan**

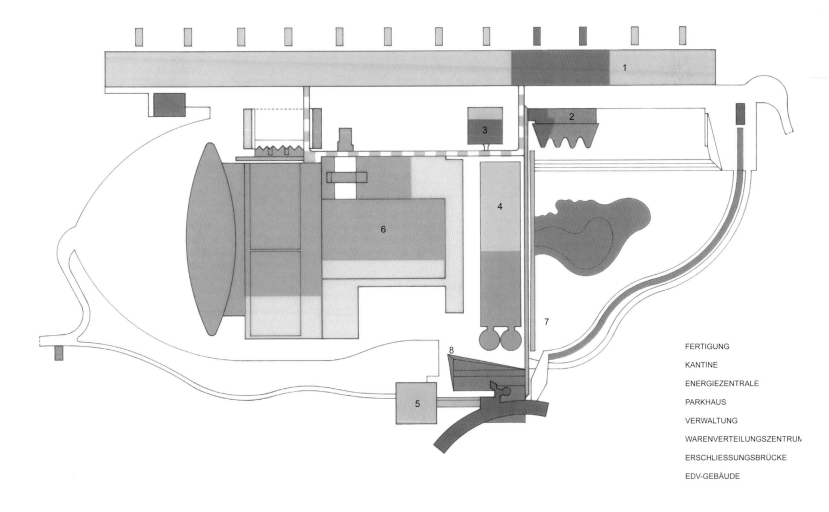

FERTIGUNG

KANTINE

ENERGIEZENTRALE

PARKHAUS

VERWALTUNG

WARENVERTEILUNGSZENTRUM

ERSCHLIESSUNGSBRÜCKE

EDV-GEBÄUDE

tecDESIGN STUDIO Los Angeles, tecARCHITECTURE Swiss AG / Sebastian Knorr, Heiko Ostmann

↑ | **Exterior view,** glass curtain wall with printed glass (front office), Ceramic Tiles (FAB)
→ | **Façade,** detail with V-columns

Inotera Headquarters
Tao Yuan

The all-glass façade, typical for standard office buildings, is reinterpreted in light of Taiwan's tradition of tile construction. An intricate assemblage of printed glass utilizing the latest glass printing technologies, structural glass and glass curtain systems, articulates the building which seeks to define its unique identity while assimilating local customs. Company A (red) and B (green) share a large clean room facility (blue) for microchip production. Whereas the office façades feed off the transparency of glass, the production spaces draw on the opacity of ceramics. Aluminum-clad steel V-columns for earthquake stabilization fasten the building to the ground.

PROJECT FACTS

Address: Tao Yuan, Taiwan, ROC. **Client:** Inotera. **Completion:** 2005. **Gross floor area:** 26,900 m². **Number of workplaces:** approx. 2000. **Main construction:** reinforced concrete. **Roof:** concrete with glass skylight at certain locations. **Lighting:** through glass façade (office building), artificial (production plant). **Main materials:** glass curtain wall. **Setting:** industrial.

↑ | **Glass façade,** office area
← | **Skylight atrium**

← | **Façade articulation** between office (red), staircase (white) and production plant (blue)
↙ | **Façade and V-columns**
↓ | **Section**

Banz + Riecks

↑ | **Production hall**
→ | **Entrance area**

Solvis Zero Emissions Factory
Brunswick

The SOLVIS project documents the cultivation of a building as part of a corporate identity in the context of maximizing sustainability. The prize-winning zero-emissions factory displays the intelligent application of energy optimization technologies for industrial construction available today. The energy demand was greatly reduced using good warmth isolation and building technology with low electricity requirements. The demand for additional energy is covered by sustainable energy, using primarily sun and biomass. A gross energy demand of 0.0 kilowatt hour per square meter is noted in the group's yearly report.

PROJECT FACTS
Address: Grotrian-Steinweg-Straße 12, 38112 Brunswick, Germany. **Planning partners:** Ingenieurbüro Burkhard Walter. **Client:** Solvis GmbH. **Completion:** 2002. **Gross floor area:** 8,500 m². **Number of workplaces:** 200. **Main construction:** wood light-weight structure. **Roof:** flat. **Lighting:** enhanced daylight optimization. **Main materials:** light wood construction with an external steel framework. **Setting:** industrial.

↑ | **Roof**, solar panels
← | **Exterior view**

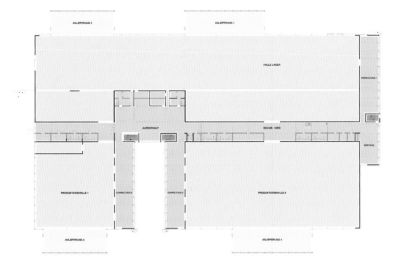

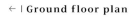

← | Ground floor plan
↙ | Elevation
↓ | Exterior

APA Kurylowicz & Associates

↑ | **Exterior**
↗ | **Façade**, detail
→ | **Entrance area**

Avon Cosmetics

Garwolin

The Avon cosmetics factory consists of several halls visually grouped around the company's name. Although all functions – organization, production and logistics – have their own building with a separate identity created by varying façades and roofs, they melt together in the common complex. The different functions can be recognized by the organization of the façades.

Address: Ulica Stacyjna 77, 08-400 Garwolin, Poland. **Other creatives:** Biuro Inzynieryjne Mostostal s.c. **Client:** AVON Operations Polska. **Completion:** 2001. **Gross floor area:** 44,768 m². **Main materials:** metal. **Setting:** rural

↑ | **Bird's-eye view**
← | **Production hall**

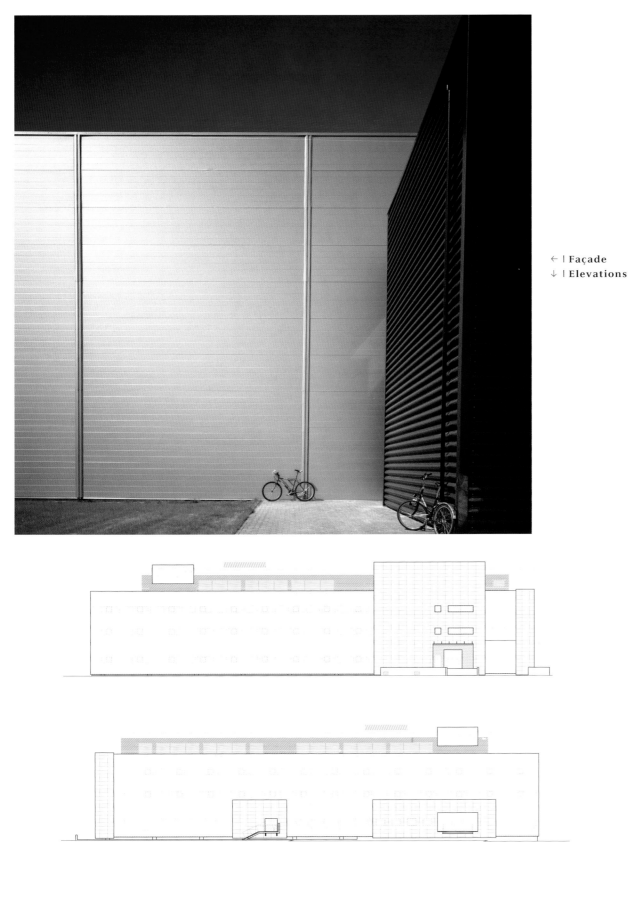

← | Façade
↓ | Elevations

seifert.stoeckmann@formal-haut with Martin Häusle

↑ | **Production hall**
↗ | **Warehouse** with cantilever roof
→ | **Open warehouse**

Elkamet
Biedenkopf

The factory complex for Elkamet, a manufacturer of plastic parts for the vehicle industry, consists of various structural units. The three production halls arranged into parallel rows are interconnected. Like other buildings, they have slightly slanted roofs that recall the surrounding hilly landscape. The warehouse, on the other hand, has an 18 meter long jutting out roof with a vigorously folded textile lining. This highly noticeable plastic element is just as programmatic for the production as the acrylic glass sinus wave along the outer walls of the warehouse. An inscription about snow is found along the edge of the roof.

PROJECT FACTS

Address: Georg-Kramer-Straße 3, 35216 Biedenkopf, Germany. **Structural engineers:** Gruppe Bau Dornbirn. **Completion:** 2000. **Gross floor area:** 3,250 m². **Number of workplaces:** 36. **Main construction:** steel frame work/profiled sheeting, aluminum sine wave RAL 9006 external. **Roof:** sloping roof (production hall), flat (warehouse). **Lighting:** daylight skylight, fluorescent tube lighting, glare reducing. **Main materials:** aluminum, steel trapezoidal sheet metal. **Setting:** rural.

IPRO DRESDEN
Planungs- und Ingenieur-
aktiengesellschaft / Carsten
Otto, Ulrich R. Schönfeld

↑ | **Lake side view**
→ | **Façade,** detail

Solarfactory Sunfilm

Großröhrsdorf / Dresden

In the Solarfactory of the Sunfilm AG, which is the first of its kind in the world, highly efficient photovoltaic thin film elements are produced in clean rooms. A building optimally adjusted to the task has been developed for the complex and constantly changing production process. One of the design aspects was to optically represent photovoltaic technology, which is currently considered one of the most dynamic technologies in the world. In addition, the heavily accented architecture of the building embodies the company's business goals and, as part of its corporate identity, makes a clear statement about the company's philosophy.

PROJECT FACTS

Address: Sunfilmstraße 8, 01900 Großröhrsdorf, Germany. **Client:** Sunfilm AG. **Completion:** 2008. **Gross floor area:** 22,000 m². **Number of workplaces:** 180. **Main construction:** reinforced concrete with steel framework. **Roof:** flat. **Lighting:** artificial illumination. **Main materials:** metal, photovoltaic elements, ESD film. **Setting:** urban.

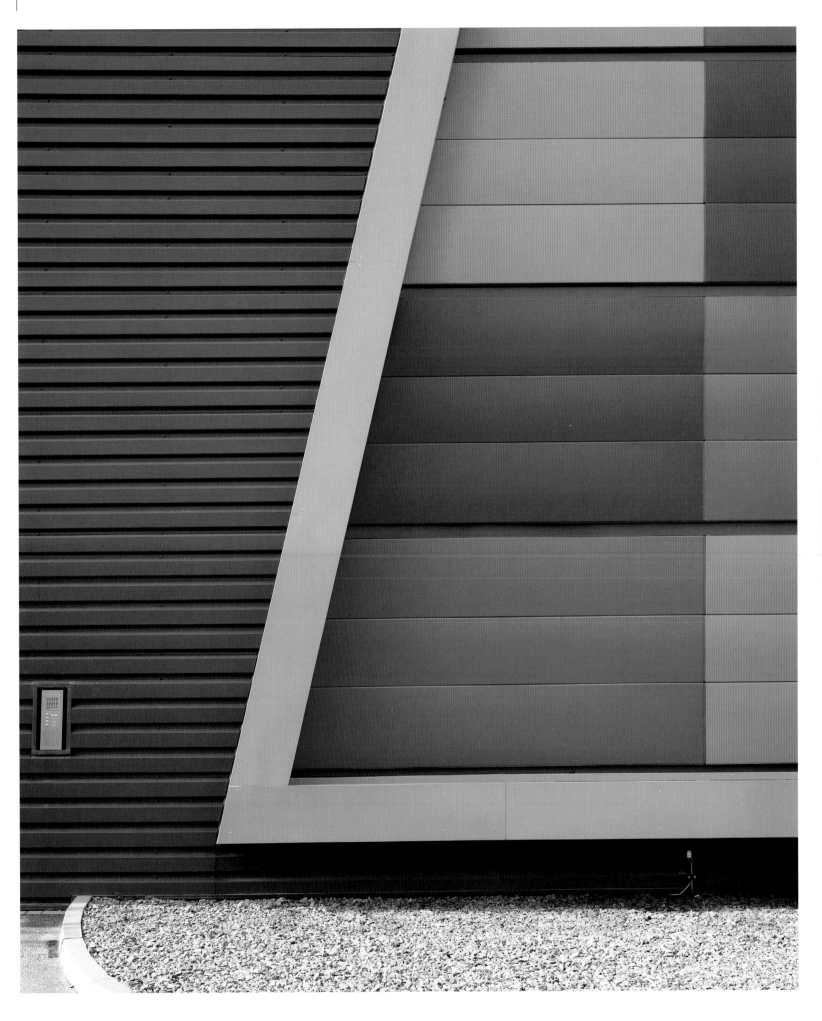

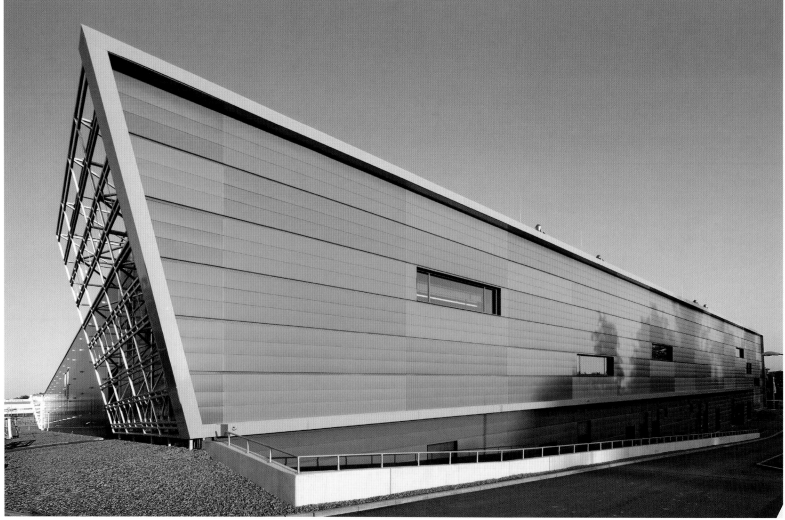

↑ | **Exterior,** dynamic architecture as an
expression of dynamic technology
← | **Production hall**

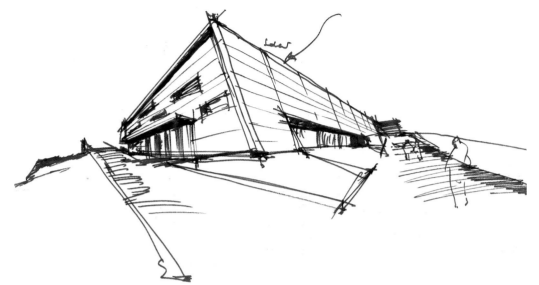

← | Sketch
↓ | Interaction between office areas and production

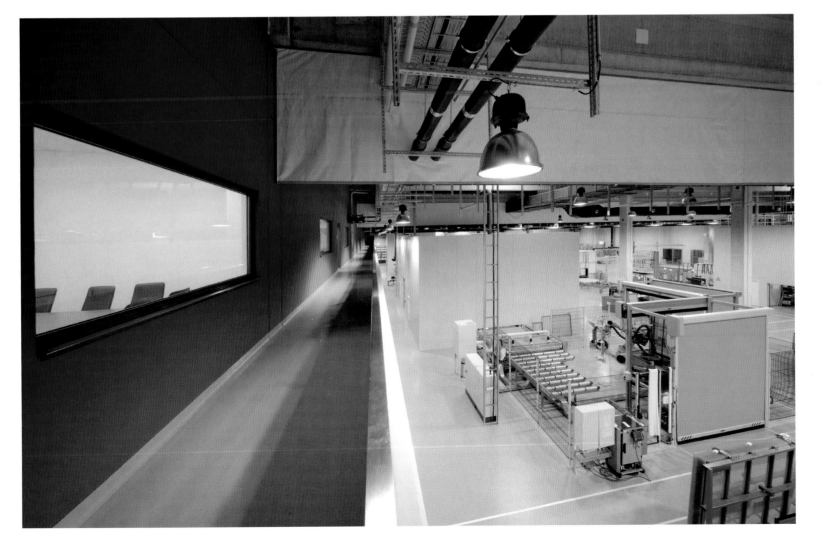

Low-
tech

Rolf Rauner
architektur + werkstätte

↑ | **View from west**
↗ | **Façade,** larch wood façade with strip windows
→ | **View from north,** front façade with door of
stainless steel

Vineyard Lackner-Tinnacher
Gamlitz

The construction of a wine cellar in 2000 supplemented the existing vineyard ensemble.
This was taken as an opportunity to reorganize the functions of the cellar and to bring it in
harmony with the existing structures. The fermentation cellar is at the center of the complex, with the other functional spaces ordered around it. The main volume consists of a
reinforced concrete cube with a support grid, offering flexibility for future development of
cellar operations. The appearance of the wine cellar is defined by the façade of untreated,
insulated larch wood lamellas on the northern and western fronts. The green roof acts as a
transition element to the natural surroundings.

PROJECT FACTS

Address: Steinbach 12, 8465 Gamlitz, Austria. **Client:** Weingut Lackner-Tinnacher. **Completion:** 2001. **Gross floor area:** 751.5 m². **Main construction:** reinforced concrete structure. **Roof:** flat. **Lighting:** daylight falling through strip windows. **Main materials:** ferroconcrete, stainless steel, larch wood. **Setting:** rural.

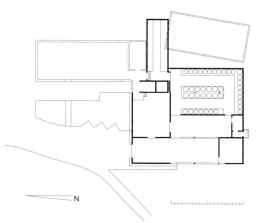

↑ | **View of roof,** greened flat roof connecting the building with the environment
← | **Transition**
↓ | **Ground floor plan**

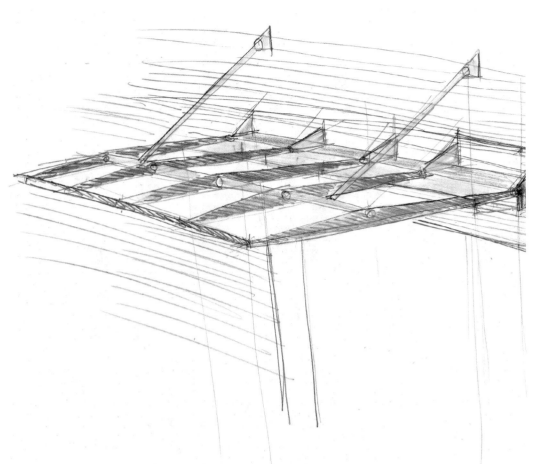

← | **Sketch,** main gate roofing
↓ | **Detail,** main gate roofing

Bernard Tschumi
Architects

↑ | **Exterior,** night view
→ | **Interior view**

Vacheron Constantin
Headquarters

Plan-les-Ouates

This building serves as the manufacturing and administrative headquarters of Switzer-land's oldest watchmaking company. The concept for the building is based on the idea of a thin, flexible double envelope. The exterior surface is sculpted using a metallic sheet that unrolls over the structure's geometry, while the interior is clad with a wood veneer. The resulting space is sleek and precise outside, warm and inviting inside. The space does not act as an enclosed object: the logic of unrolling permits abundant light to enter on the north side and admits filtered light on the south, while opening itself to welcome workers and visitors to the facilities.

PROJECT FACTS

Address: Chemin du Tourbillon 10, 1228 Plan-les-Ouates, Switzerland. **Client:** Vacheron Constantin, Richemont, Intl. **Completion:** 2004. **Gross floor area:** 10,250 m². **Number of workplaces:** 325. **Main construction:** steel frame. **Roof:** curved metal skin. **Lighting:** through façade and light well. **Main materials:** perforated steel, perforated cherry wood panels, glass for circulation. **Setting:** rural.

↑ | **Exterior,** view from west
← | **Atrium**

← | **Interior,** view of workstations
↓ | **Sections through atrium**

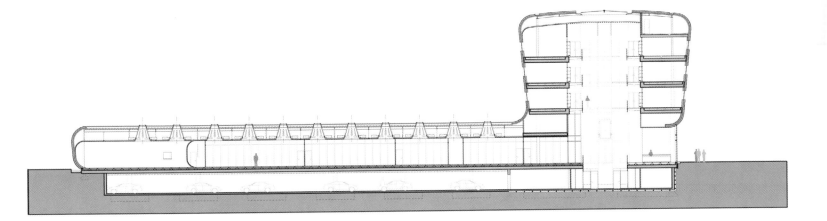

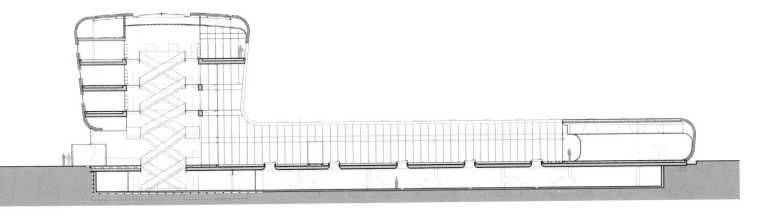

Manuelle Gautrand
architecture

↑ | **Cold storage**, unit 4
↗ | **Cold storage**, unit 1
↗↗ | **Ground floor plan**
→ | **Exterior view**

Airport Catering

Nantes

This catering facility is used for the storage, preparation and packaging of in-flight meals and drinks served on aircraft departing Nantes-Atlantique airport. The aim was to simplify and hide all the interior complexity. The building is divided into two strips: one for general handling and storing of non-perishable foodstuffs, the other for cold rooms and kitchens. The first is seven meters wide with blue-tinted polycarbonate panel walls and has a unified, cool atmosphere. By contrast, the other, where food is prepared and packaged, is five meters wide and mostly in concrete. The cold storage units are covered by oversized colored decals that indicate what type of food is kept inside.

PROJECT FACTS Address: Nantes Airport, Nantes, France. **Client:** Actair. **Completion:** 1998. **Gross floor area:** 1,200 m². **Number of workplaces:** 20. **Main construction:** steel. **Roof:** flat. **Lighting:** through façade and through roof. **Main materials:** concrete, polycarbonate panels. **Setting:** industrial.

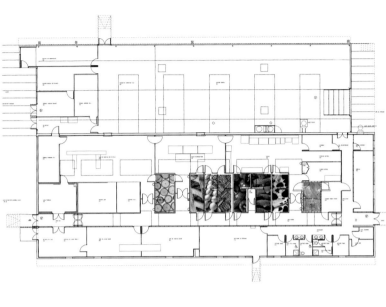

Philippe Samyn and Partners,
architects & engineers

↑ | **Exterior view** by night
→ | **Interior**

Forestry Branch
Marche-en-Famenne

The Forestry Branch in the heart of the Ardennes Forest houses the treatment process of
sylviculture grains. The irregular polygon shape of the site, timbered with 200-year-old
oaks, made the choice of a compact ovoid form obvious. A framework of composed arches
constitutes the structure which covers the whole building. Two secondary buildings are
placed inside this shell. They house the cold storage, administrative rooms and laborato-
ries. The central nave is reserved for large machines which treat and pre-dry grain. The
basic element of the structure is a double layered-arch composed of various rectangular
wood elements. The building is covered with tiles of laminated reflecting glass.

Address: Zoning industriel de Aye, rue André Ferer, 5400 Marche-en-Famenne, Belgium.
Client: Exécutif Régional Wallon. **Completion:** 1995. **Gross floor area:** 1,144 m². **Setting:** rural.

↑ | **Interior**
← | **Exterior**

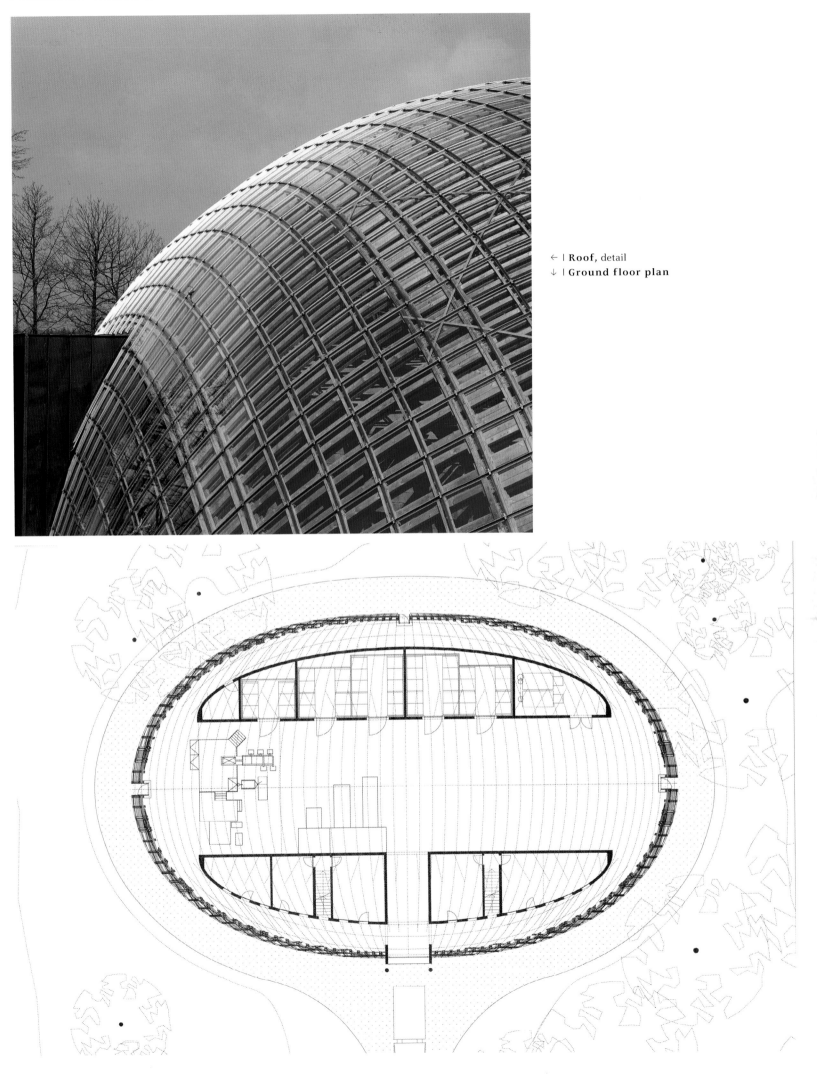

← | **Roof**, detail
↓ | **Ground floor plan**

BVN Architecture –
Bligh Voller Nield/
Susanne Mayer, Abbie
Galvin, Micha Hinden

↑ | **Front façade,** old and new elements create
the characteristic face of the building

Wilkhahn Asia Pacific Factory

Alexandria

The collocation of the Wilkhahn Asia Pacific factory and showroom has been used strategically to demonstrate Wilkhahn's holistic approach to the process – products are part of a life cycle, which is given expression in the project. The border between factory and showroom, production and display has been blurred. A dramatic ramp leads through the factory, enabling the progression of manufacture and assembly to be understood, and letting the movement, sounds and smells of the manufacturing process be experienced. The seamless detailing of dramatic new elements and the organic quality of the birch finish contrasts with the industrial steel structure of the existing warehouse.

Address: 35–39 Bourke Road, A2, Alexandria Industrial Estate, 42–62 Maddox Street, Alexandria NSW 2015, Australia. **Client:** Wilkhahn Asia Pacific. **Completion:** 2006. **Gross floor area:** 2,500 m². **Number of workplaces:** 22. **Main construction:** steel frame work with brick filling. **Roof:** steel truss and metal deck saw tooth roof. **Lighting:** daylight through roof and façade. **Main materials:** existing brickwork, birch plywood, painted brickwork/plasterboard. **Setting:** industrial.

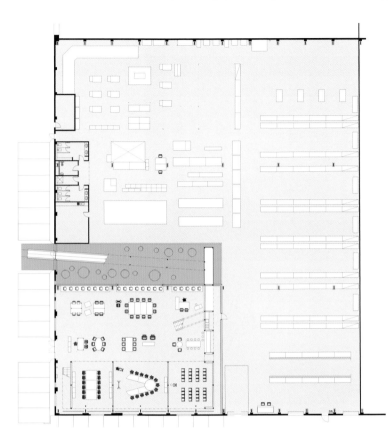

↑ | **Ground floor plan**
↓ | **Ramp,** entry to the showroom via dramatic
ramp through factory

↑ | **Platform,** forms a mezzanine for sales staff
and a stair allows descent onto the showroom floor

Architekten.3P
Feuerstein Rüdenauer
& Partner /
Gerhard Feuerstein

↑ | **View of old and new building**

Feuerstein Windows
Oberstaufen

In the course of the expansion and reorganization of the window factory, a new low-cost wood structure has been added. The new building docks seamlessly onto the existing machine room and offers ground-level area for final assembly of window and façade elements. The closed façades were consciously fashioned similar to the traditional houses in the area, clad with three layers of white fir shingles. A tried-and-true rear ventilation system was used. The building features cellars under a portion of the floor surface, providing adequate storage space. A gallery level houses management offices, showroom and space for employees. The new building opens itself to the street using generous glass surfaces. Immobile wood lamellas provide necessary sun protection on the west front, creating a pleasant, honey-colored illumination inside. The structure was prefabricated as a wood frame and assembled on site in three days.

PROJECT FACTS

Address: Mühlenstraße 5, 87534 Oberstaufen, Germany. **Client:** Fensterbau Feuerstein, Herbert Feuerstein. **Completion:** 2007. **Gross floor area:** 580 m². **Number of workplaces:** 10. **Main construction:** timber frame construction. **Roof:** flat roof. **Lighting:** daylight falling through wooden fins in the façade, roof lights. **Main materials:** silver fir timber, glass. **Setting:** rural.

↑ | **Detail of façade,** timber fins and shingles
↙ | **Plans**

↓ | **Interior,** view from gallery level

crossboundaries
architects

↑ | **Green roof,** view from dormitory onto the
green roof
↗ | **View from street**
→ | **Corridor,** next to the production line

Aimer Lingerie Factory
Beijing

The design of the Aimer Lingerie production center is based on two ground principles:
Firstly, on the idea of "self-presentation" in order to project the idea of the company to
the outside world, and secondly, the principle of layering various functions on top of one
another. An accessible green roof completely covers the platform story containing warehouse and distribution. The "presentation area" includes production and assembly, as well
as space for personnel. This includes a cafeteria and a leisure sports complex. These functions, located on one story, have a transparent outer envelope that makes them accessible
and visible from the outside.

PROJECT FACTS

Address: Mapuo Economy & Industry Zone, Shunyi District, Beijing, China. **Planning partners:** BIAD (Beijing Institute of Architectural Design) as LDI (Local Design Institute). **Client:** Aimer Lingerie Co. Ltd. **Completion:** 2010. **Gross floor area:** 46,000 m². **Number of workplaces:** 600. **Main construction:** reinforced concrete. **Roof:** accessible green roof, flat. **Lighting:** natural through glass façade, artificial. **Main materials:** glass, drywall, cement floor. **Setting:** industrial.

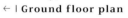
↑ | **Lobby,** entrance area
← | **Ground floor plan**

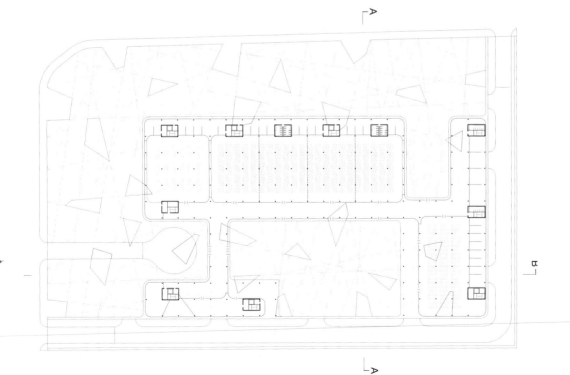

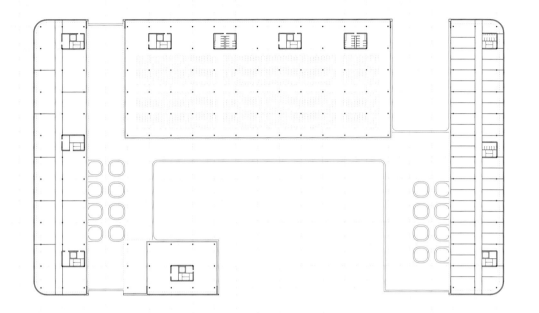

← | Second floor plan
↓ | View from canteen

Patrick Berger et Jacques
Anziutti Architectes

↑ | **East front**
↗ | **Refectory**
→ | **North front**

Leather Goods Factory
Ardennes

The new handbag factory plays on the renowned name of the company manufacturing luxury items. Working conditions are above average and attempt to infuse the company with quality of life. The building's visible frame translates the manual means of production into architecture. The entrance is found in a perpendicular wing, which also offers access to administration and restaurant and can be used for hosting events. The 720 ton steel structure appears nearly monolithic, without revealing any apparent expansion joints.

PROJECT FACTS

Address: Ardennes, France. **Landscaping:** Michel Desvigne. **Client:** confidential. **Completion:** 2004. **Gross floor area:** 5,466 m². **Main construction:** steel framework. **Roof:** flat. **Lighting:** through façade and roof. **Main materials:** aluminum, glass, wood. **Setting:** rural.

↑ | **East front**
← | **Gallery**

← | Gallery
↓ | Ground floor plan

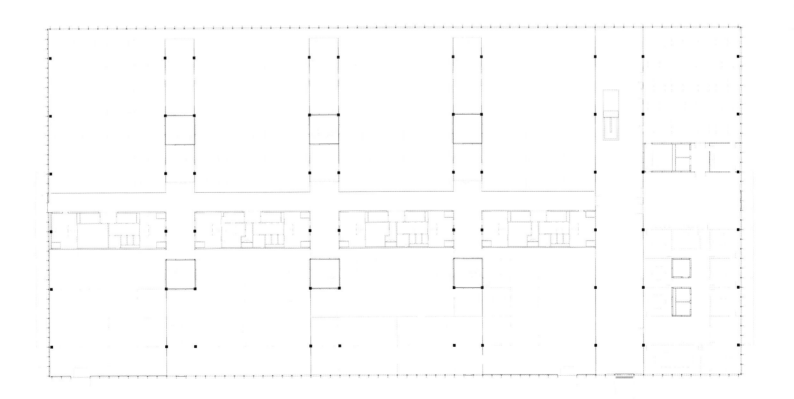

Melkan Gursel &
Murat Tabanlioglu

↑ | **Foyer,** clearly structured entrance area

Tunacelik Factory
Istanbul

The design of the overall structure developed from the surrounding area's functional and utilization requirements. The open office system leads onto the showroom floor. Unlike the factory section of the complex, the showroom area has been designed with more flexible architectural capabilities. In addition to the moving lights above the factory, the roof lighting on the showroom outlines the geometrical lines of that building and acts as a transition from the showroom area to the office floors. Compared to the factory, the showroom building is a more translucent body and the green area directly in front of this building acts to carry the outer world into the inner space of the building itself.

PROJECT FACTS

Address: Kinali Mevkii, 34947 Silivri Istanbul, Turkey. **Client:** Tunaçelik Esya Sanayi ve Ticaret A.S.
Completion: 2002. **Gross floor area:** 23,250 m². **Number of workplaces:** 150. **Main construction:** steel
framework. **Roof:** flat. **Lighting:** through roof and artifical in the factory, through façade and artificial
in the showroom. **Main materials:** steel, glass, aluminum. **Setting:** industrial.

↑ | **Showroom,** spacious showroom to view all
the goods at once.
↙ | **Section**

↑ | **Production hall,** design of overall structure
developed out of the functional and utilization
requirements of the area
↓ | **Ground floor plan**

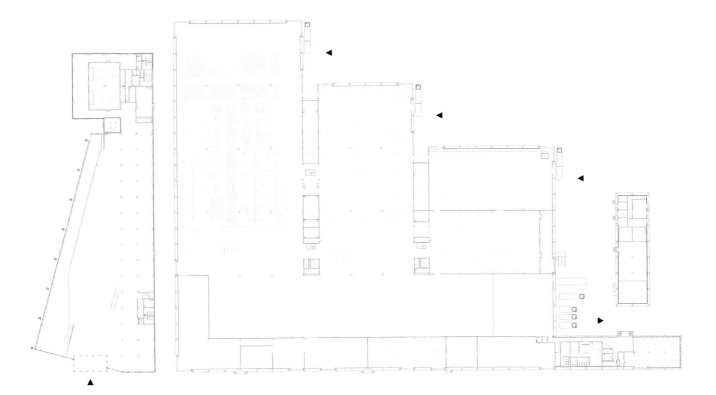

↑ | **Main access**
→ | **Corridor,** lobby to auditorium

Nestlé Chocolate Factory Museum
Paseo Tollocan

Nestlé's chocolate factory in Mexico City was in need of an inner pathway for visitors to witness the production of their favorite chocolates. The idea wqas to create the first chocolate museum in Mexico and have a 300 meter long façade along the motorway as the new image of the factory was born. The first phase required a 634 meter squared space that could accommodate the main entrance for the visitors to start their voyage into the chocolate factory. As soon as they enter this playful yet striking space, they would be greeted by the reception area, the theater, where they would be prepared for the Nestlé experience, the store or museum shop, and the passage to the tunnel inside the old existing factory.

PROJECT FACTS **Address:** Carretera México – Toluca, Paseo Tollocan, km 62.3, Mexico. **Client:** Nestlé México. **Completion:** 2007. **Gross floor area:** 634 m². **Main construction:** steel framework, cladded with alu-zinc panel. **Roof:** multi-shed roof. **Lighting:** artificial. **Main materials:** color deck, 0.5 mm aluzinc Hunter Douglas panel, sheet rock panel. **Setting:** industrial.

↑ | **Façade of auditorium**
← | **Entrance area**

← | **Lobby**
↓ | **Sections**

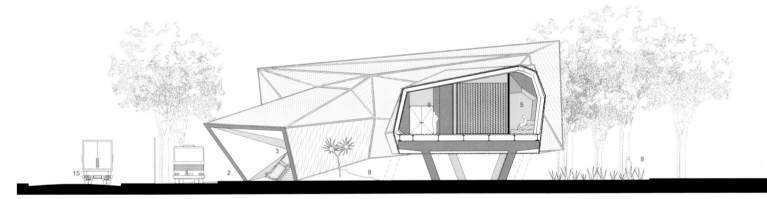

1 motor lobby   6 museum shop
2 drop off   8 landscaping
3 acces   15 Leonardo DaVinci street
5 auditorium

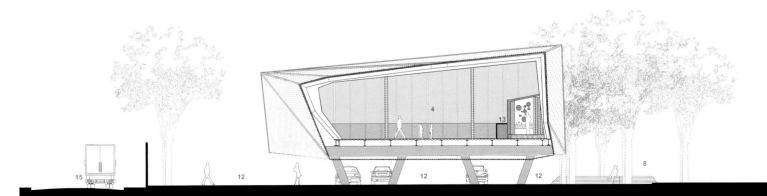

4 lobby   13 reception
7 restrooms   15 Leonardo DaVinci street
8 landscaping
12 employee parking

Sandrolini Architecte /
Jean-Marc Sandrolini

↑ | **General view,** building embedded in the landscape
→ | **Exterior view**

Louis Vuitton
Conde (Indre)

The building is located in the midst of large cereal crop plains interspersed with some wooded areas. The landscape was at the heart Sof the architectural concept. The project is structured along an internal axis bathed in abundant natural daylight, connected to a large glass workshop, the offices, facility rooms and a large glass cylindrical restaurant which is the complex's only curved feature. The transparency of the façades and the openings in the roof make daylight an essential element of the project. The ceiling is extended to the outside, below the roofing which gives the building a slight floating aspect. The building enhances the landscape by re-enforcing its horizontal lines and harmony.

Address: Conde (Indre), France. **Client:** Louis Vuitton. **Completion:** 2002. **Gross floor area:** 8,000 m². **Number of workplaces:** 250. **Main construction:** steel framework. **Roof:** shed. **Lighting:** through roof and façades. **Main materials:** aluminum, glass, steel. **Setting:** rural.

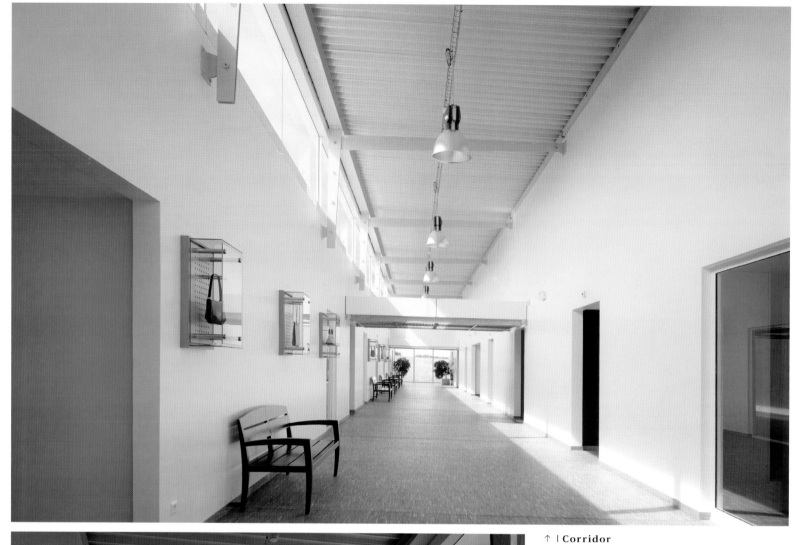

↑ | Corridor
← | Interior view
↓ | Model master view

← | **Production hall**
↓ | **Site,** night view

Cuno Brullmann
Jean-Luc Crochon
+ Associés

↑ | **Perspective**
↗ | **Parking**
→ | **Aerial view**
→→| **Plans,** ground and first floor plan

Micro-tech Plant

Gals

In addition to simply responding to an industrial process, the determining factor of this project was its integration into the landscape and its dialogue with nature. The volumes are assembled along the road to make it possible "to plant" the building vis-à-vis its environment. The angular geometry permits access to the offices via the roof which responds to both technical and architectural constraints. This industrial pragmatism leads to a purity of design.

Address: Bernstrasse 5, 2076 Gals, Switzerland. **Other creatives:** Burckhardt and Partner, J-Marc Weill. **Client:** Unitechnologies Group MTA / Sysmelec. **Completion:** 2002. **Gross floor area:** 6,000 m². **Main construction:** concrete, steel. **Roof:** steel-shed. **Lighting:** natural. **Main materials:** stainless steel super roof: steel and glass cladding, rough concrete. **Setting:** rural.

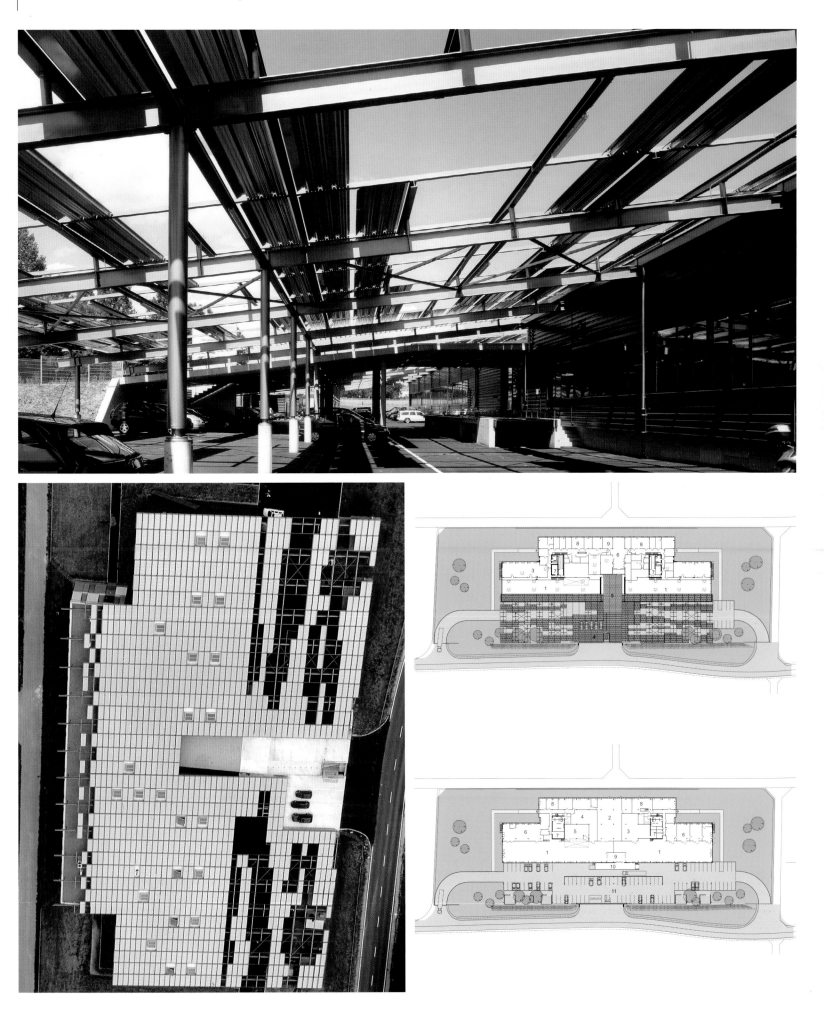

↑ | **Façade,** view by night
→ | **Side elevation** with parking area

Rexam

Ludesch

Rexam, one of the world's leading producers of consumer packaging, built this drinks
can production plant as a "wall to wall" operation adjacent to a filling plant at Ludesch
in Vorarlberg. In order to create a scale appropriate for the location, ATP Architects and
Engineers highlighted the production line running across the entire complex and gave the
volumes of the building the same external form, allowing them to be read as individual
elements. The resulting three-dimensional implementation of the "functional joint" concept in the architectural and engineering projects is the result of a coordinated integrated
design process.

Address: Illweg, 6713 Ludesch, Austria. **Client:** Rexam Beverage Can Enzesfeld GmbH. **Completion:** 2007. **Gross floor area:** 19,300 m². **Main construction:** prefabricated reinforced concrete columns. **Roof:** flat with laminated timber beams, aluminum sheets, thermal insulation. **Lighting:** natural and artificial. **Main materials:** profiled aluminum façade elements, light grey bituminous slate roofing. **Setting:** rural.

Endo Shuhei Architect
Institute

↑ | **South-east side**

Rooftecture U

Setouchi City

The premises of the railroad brake shoe factory and an affiliated institution are located in a typical Japanese farm village zone, where a rice field spreads out without bounds and a mountain looks like a distant place. A difference in grade with the ridge of the two sections of the incline roofs was made in order to set the volume on some kind of border. This arrangement was adopted to establish the surface of a wall which had a southern orientation at the central upper part of the factory. Intense sideways light and a louver window for ventilation were installed on this front in order to create pleasant and comfortable work conditions with sufficient illumination and ventilation.

PROJECT FACTS

Address: 232-1, Kitajima Aza Sekimen Oku-cho Setouchi City, Okayama-pref., Japan. **Client:** Ueda Brake Co.,Ltd. **Completion:** 2008. **Gross floor area:** 2,238 m². **Main construction:** steel framework. **Roof:** shed. **Main materials:** galvanized steel sheets, neo panels. **Setting:** rural.

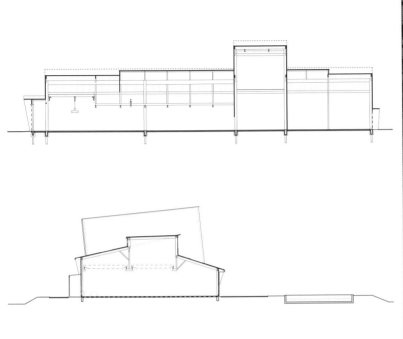

↑ | Sections
↓ | Production hall

↑ | Production hall

↑ | **Exterior**
↗ | **Façade**
↗↗ | **Edge of the building**
→ | **Interior,** design draft office building

Karcoma Fixtures
Sindelfingen-Maichingen

In order to create a representative appearance, the new fixture manufacturer's building was created by combining volumes for production and administration. Contrastingly designed façades make both areas discernable from the outside. In the administrative area, the building roof rolls upwards and gives the complex its dynamic lightness. The room organization is informed by the latest developments, optimizing the circulation and material flow through the building complex arranged in a parallel fashion.

Address: Stuttgarter Straße 51, 71069 Sindelfingen-Maichingen, Germany. **Client:** Karcoma.
Completion: 2005. **Gross floor area:** 2,500 m². **Main construction:** solid reinforced concrete
structure / steel framework. **Main materials:** glass, plaster, metal. **Setting:** industrial.

↑ | **Restaurant** from kitchen side
→ | **Restaurant** from outside

Kinosaki Beer Factory
GUBI-GABU

Kinosaki

Located on the Maruyama River near the famous Kinosaki hot springs, this local beer factory facility with a restaurant is divided into three volumes along the water. Each of these volumes opens up onto the view that was made famous by Naoya Shiga's novel "At Kinosaki". Each volume is defined and formed by people's movement, transformed by the internal factor of the audience's zone distribution. While movements become lines, their intersection creates reverse images of the scenery. The factory becomes a catalyst to the recognition of topography.

PROJECT FACTS

Address: Kuruhi, Kinosaki-cho, Toyooka-shi, Hyogo 6696115, Japan. **Client:** Japanese-style hotel "Yamamoto-ya". **Completion:** 1998. **Gross floor area:** 279,000 m². **Main construction:** reinforced concrete and steel. **Roof:** one side shed. **Lighting:** artificial and through façade. **Main materials:** exposed concrete, corrugated sheet glass, corrugated sheet aluminum, teflon-coated membrane. **Setting:** rural.

↑ | **Façade** at night
← | **Factory** at night

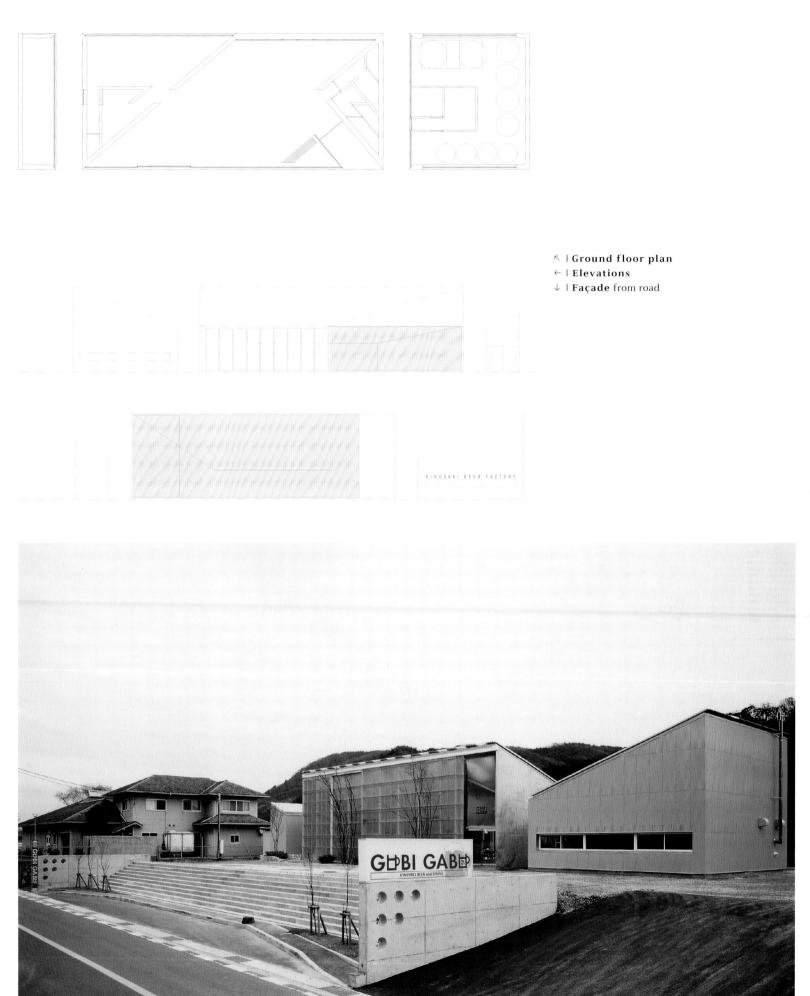

↖ | Ground floor plan
← | Elevations
↓ | Façade from road

↑ | **South façade,** automatically controlled glass lamellas
→ | **Exterior,** north-east elevation

Multifunctional Building
Herrenberg

The building acts as a keystone to comprehensive reconstruction measures taken at the historic company facility located at the train station. Production, administration and exhibition areas are found in this multifunctional industrial building. The basic form consists of a fair-faced concrete frame, into which a glass cube has been inserted. Three material types characterize the building: fair-faced concrete, glass and metal. The clear form sees itself as an antipode to the historically expanded industrial ensemble, a dialog of functional architecture spanning centuries. Energy supply takes place via warmth pumps, and the sprinkler tank additionally serves as a warmth buffer for attenuating top loads.

PROJECT FACTS

Address: Bahnhofstraße 25, 71083 Herrenberg, Germany. **Client:** Walter Knoll AG & Co.KG. **Completion:** 2006. **Gross floor area:** 6,700 m². **Number of workplaces:** 110. **Main construction:** reinforced concrete. **Roof:** flat. **Lighting:** through façade. **Main materials:** concrete, glass, aluminum. **Setting:** urban.

↑ | **Façade,** as communications area
← | **View from the foyer**

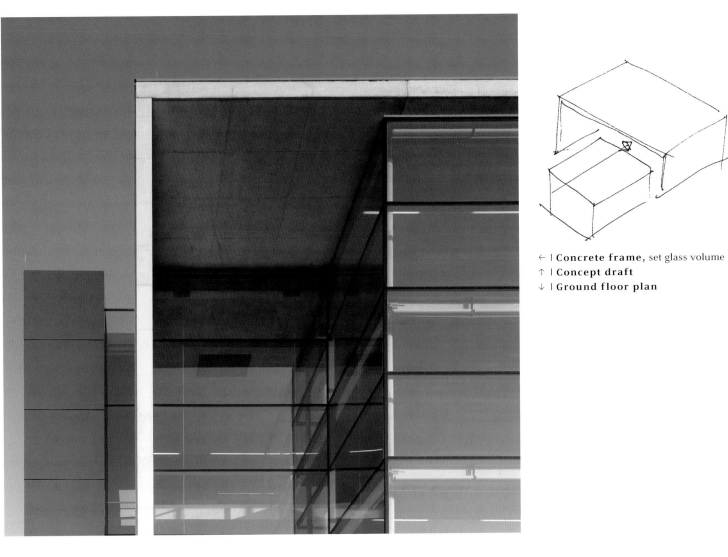

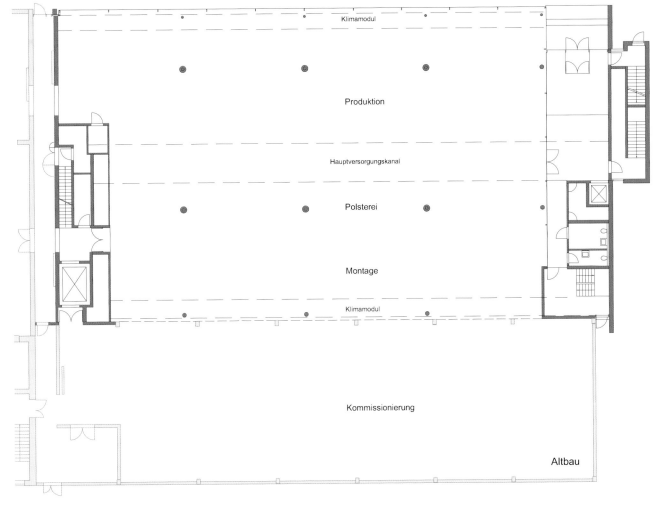

← | **Concrete frame,** set glass volume
↑ | **Concept draft**
↓ | **Ground floor plan**

Klimamodul

Produktion

Hauptversorgungskanal

Polsterei

Montage

Klimamodul

Kommissionierung

Altbau

↑ | **Front elevation** with entrance area

Fifth Town Artisan Cheese Factory

Picton

The Cheese Company produces hand-made goat and sheep milk cheeses. The cheeses and the building are both characterized by quality and harmony with the environment. As a result, the building is slated to become Canada's first LEED Platinum factory. The facility and its grounds are open to the public for educational purposes as well as retail sales. "Folding over" the conventionally linear production process into a contained area behind a glass wall, the architects solved the challenge of revealing the manufacturing activities to the public while also ensuring that the facility was cost-effective, energy efficient and compliant with government health and safety regulations.

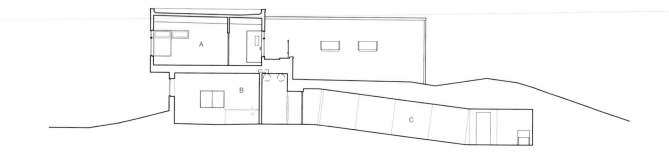

PROJECT FACTS

Address: 4309 County Road 8 R. R. #4, Picton, ON, Canada. **Client:** Petra Cooper of the Fifth Town Artisan Cheese Co. **Completion:** 2008. **Gross floor area:** 4,200 m². **Number of workplaces:** 1. **Main construction:** durisol structural block made from recycled wood waste chips and filled with 50% slag concrete. **Roof:** flat. **Lighting:** retail windows, solar PV panels. **Main materials:** galvalume metal sheeting and reclaimed timber siding. **Setting:** rural.

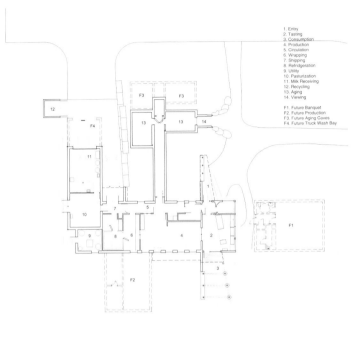

1. Entry
2. Tasting
3. Consumption
4. Production
5. Circulation
6. Wrapping
7. Shipping
8. Refridgeration
9. Utility
10. Pasturization
11. Milk Receiving
12. Recycling
13. Aging
14. Viewing

F1. Future Banquet
F2. Future Production
F3. Future Aging Caves
F4. Future Truck Wash Bay

↑ | **Main entrance**
↙ | **Section,** shows connection between manufac-
turing spaces and buried aging caves

↑ | **Ground floor plan**
↓ | **South elevation,** reveals programmatic
arrangement

Storages

etc.

Manuelle Gautrand
architecture

↑ | Interior

A12 Warehouse

Gennevilliers Harbor

The 12.5 meter height of the building is divided up into two parts: a base wall, 5.8 meter high in polished dark grey concrete that is fit to resist wear and tear, and a translucent upper part. The idea is to bring in as much daylight as possible into a space that may one day house workshops or production lines. The translucent upper shell is made of cellular polycarbonate sheets, organized in five layers – 16 millimeter thick in total. By day it brings in abundant light and reflects the colors of the sky; by night, it lights up from within like a lantern. It floats like a fabric of luminous prisms stretched twelve meters above the work spaces, providing a wealth of changing lights.

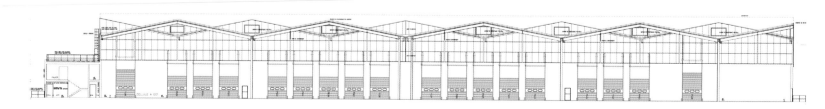

PROJECT FACTS

Address: Môle 2, Gennevilliers Harbor, France. **Client:** Port autonome de Paris. **Completion:** 1999. **Gross floor area:** 10,000 m². **Number of workplaces:** 20. **Main construction:** steel. **Roof:** shed. **Lighting:** through translucent upper shell. **Main materials:** base wall in dark grey concrete, upper shell in cellular polycarbonate sheets. **Setting:** industrial.

↑ | Exterior view
↙ | Section

↓ | Façade

Khanna Schultz

↑ | Interior view
↗ | Loading dock
→ | Exterior view

Writer Warehouse: Delhi

Haryana

Maximizing storage area within zoning constraints was a major design concern. The façades are composed of angled fins that bring a soft oblique light into the spaces and circular pre-cast concrete glazed tubes that project from the façade and cut heat and glare while bringing light in. The internal organization of the building is simple; a central loading dock where trailers unload is flanked by storage spaces on either side. The spaces are filled with a multi-level steel racking system. Given the budget, time frame and available building technologies, the building does not rely on fine detailing and finishing. Instead it attempts to give a robust, tectonic form to a discrete set of ideas.

PROJECT FACTS **Address:** National Highway 8, Gurgaon, Haryana, India. **Client:** Writer Corporation. **Completion:** 2004. **Gross floor area:** 6,400 m². **Number of workplaces:** approx. 40. **Main construction:** concrete frame structure. **Roof:** flat. **Lighting:** daylight through façade and artificial light. **Main materials:** concrete poured in place and block. **Setting:** industrial.

↑ | **Interior,** façade detail
← | **Interior view,** high bay warehouse

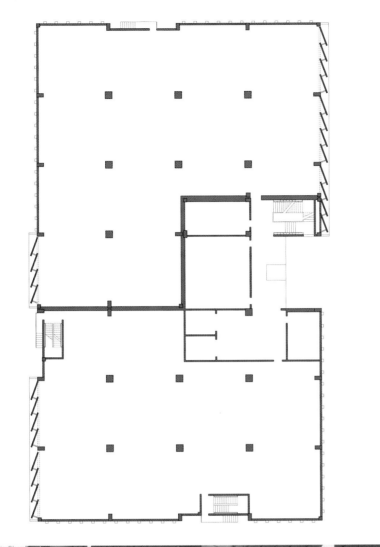

← | **Ground floor plan**
↓ | **Interior,** façade detail

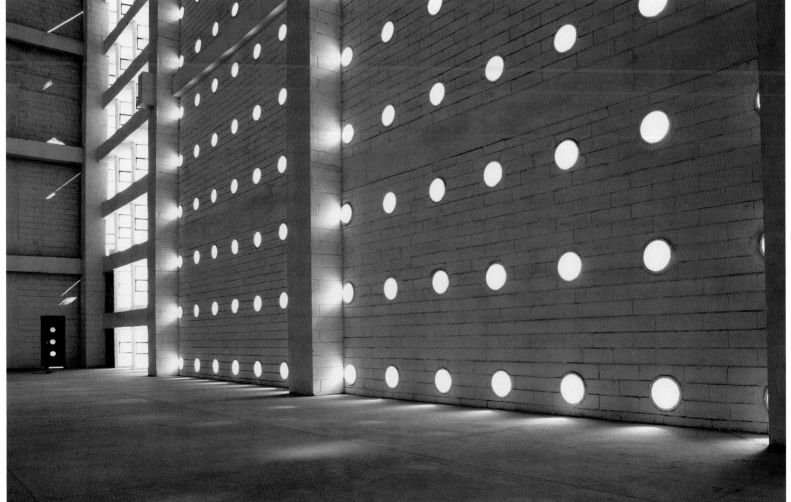

Khanna Schultz

↑ | **Exterior views**
↗ | **Interior,** wall detail
→ | **Interior**
→→| **Section** at projecting panel

Writer Warehouse: Mumbai

Navi Mumbai

This façade is conceived as a transmitter of daylight, minimizing the requirement for artificial lighting while also managing the intense heat and glare of the summer sun. The skin of the building is divided into vertical strips which fold outward in an alternating rhythm, allowing diffuse light to slip sideways into the large volume. The construction of the folds in the façade posed the major structural and constructional challenge in the project. The final method was to create the folds from a series of welded metal plates that would be sprayed with gunite and then plastered smooth, allowing for speed of construction and a precision that would be difficult to achieve in pre-cast concrete.

PROJECT FACTS

Address: Mahape, Navi Mumbai, India. **Client:** Writer Corporation. **Completion:** 2007. **Gross floor area:** 6,300 m². **Main construction:** concrete frame with steel plate infill. **Roof:** flat. **Lighting:** daylight through façade and artificial light. **Main materials:** in-situ concrete, steel plates with spray concrete. **Setting:** industrial.

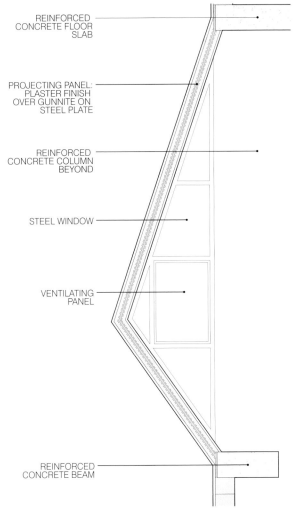

REINFORCED CONCRETE FLOOR SLAB

PROJECTING PANEL: PLASTER FINISH OVER GUNNITE ON STEEL PLATE

REINFORCED CONCRETE COLUMN BEYOND

STEEL WINDOW

VENTILATING PANEL

REINFORCED CONCRETE BEAM

| Khanna Schultz

↑ | **Interior view**
↗ | **Roof detail**, interior
→ | **Exterior view**

Writer Warehouse: Chennai
Vandallur

The massing for this warehouse was dictated by zoning requirements and the client's need to maximize storage area. As a reaction to the small, conventionally scaled windows on the factories and storage facilities around the site, the architects created façades that act as transmitters of ambient light. The client was interested in managing the intense heat and glare of the summer sun to limit the need for artificial cooling. This warehouse has large 14 square meter fins that detach from the face of the building to allow movement of soft light into the space. In the rear structure, horizontal bands of masonry are separated by thin inset glazed slots through which light seeps into the building.

PROJECT FACTS

Address: National Highway 45, Vandallur, Tamil Nadu, India. **Client:** Writer Corporation. **Completion:** 2003. **Gross floor area:** 4,800 m². **Number of workplaces:** approx. 40. **Main construction:** concrete frame with block infill. **Roof:** flat. **Lighting:** daylight through façade and artificial light. **Main materials:** in-situ concrete. **Setting:** industrial.

↑ | **Interior view**
← | **Exterior**

← | **Façade,** windows
↓ | **Ground floor plan**

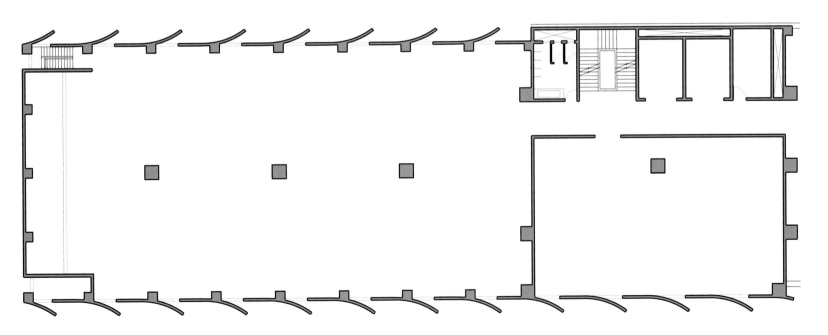

Ehrlich Architects

↑ | **Entrance**
↗ | **Exterior,** burnished concrete, Cor-ten steel
and channel glass clad the exterior of the building
→ | **Pump house**

Warehouse Campus Expansion
Santa Fe Springs

This project added approximately 30,000 square meters of additional shipping, distribution, and warehousing capacity to an existing warehouse facility built in 1984. The addition dramatically improves the work environment for hundreds of employees by providing access to natural light and ventilation. A 244 meter long "main street," punctuated by skylights, bamboo gardens and lounges connects two new entrances and "nodes" with employee break areas. A walking track encircles the 17 hectare site that has been newly land- and hardscaped, featuring drought-tolerant California native plants and bioswaled parking lots.

PROJECT FACTS **Address:** Santa Fe Springs, CA, USA. **Client:** confidential. **Completion:** 2006. **Gross floor area:** 30,000 m². **Number of workplaces:** confidential. **Main construction:** tilt-up concrete construction. **Roof:** single-ply membrane. **Lighting:** through channel glass façade, roof skylights and artificial lighting. **Main materials:** channel glass, Cor-ten steel, burnished concrete block, insulated metal panels. **Setting:** industrial.

↑ | **Exterior of the building,** burnished concrete, Cor-ten steel and channel glass clad
← | **Channel glass** allow natural light to penetrate the warehouse

← | **Interior,** "main street" connects various departments

↓ | **Ground floor plan**

existing

new

O.F.D.A. / Taku Sakaushi +
Takeshi Nakashima

↑ | **Exterior view,** diagonal columns support
vertical and horizontal load
→ | **Exterior view,** edge of an office and
monolithic support

Re-Tem Corporation

Tokyo

This plant shreds mechanical products into metals and plastics. Architectural strategy
was to reveal the flow of materials using a discrete layout: small shiny metal covered
volumes for each facility, a large astylar stock yard with diagonal posts and three-layered
building for work section, storage and office. The meandering shape of the second layer
is brought about by the engineering consideration. The triagonal polyhedron spans more
than 15 meters. It is painted with four colors that were sampled out of human skin and
patterned using a mathematical algorithm. Added small pieces of thin glass with other
patterns create an impression of delicate skin.

PROJECT FACTS **Address:** Jonanjima 3-2-9, 143-0002, Ohta-ku, Tokyo, Japan. **Client:** Re-Tem corporation. **Completion:** 2005. **Gross floor area:** 3,994 m². **Main construction:** steel framework. **Roof:** flat. **Lighting:** through façade, light well, artificial (office), through façade, artificial (factory). **Main materials:** glass cladding over painted fiber cement board (office), punched stainless steel, plate, painted gypsum board (plant). **Setting:** industrial.

↑ | **Interior view,** office with windows laid out discretely
← | **Layout plan**

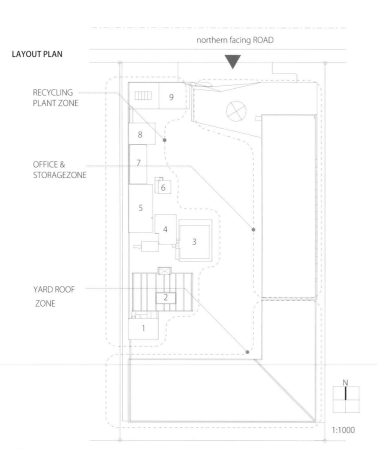

LAYOUT PLAN

northern facing ROAD

RECYCLING
PLANT ZONE

OFFICE &
STORAGEZONE

YARD ROOF
ZONE

9

8

7

6

5

4

3

2

1

N

1:1000

← | **Office** with a light well
↓ | **Staircase** at an entrance

b&k+ brandlhuber & co

↑ | **Front elevation,** Dönges part
↗ | **Side elevation,** Dönges part
→ | **Side elevation,** Cramer part

Standard+

Cologne

Two industrial buildings were added to an existing centrally located commercial complex with a challenging plot arrangement. Material selection and façade design give each building a unique, practical identity, simultaneously creating a formal unity for the entire building group. Thus, glass was used for the glaziery, wood rind for the carpentry shop, and plastic for the dental lab. The construction was adjusted with various span lengths and story heights to the demands of production and administration. Various glass fronts react accordingly to the warmth, noise and sun protection conditions.

PROJECT FACTS **Address:** Pasteurstraße/Boltensternstraße, 50735 Cologne, Germany. **Client:** Family Dönges, Family Cramer, Jens Wentzsche. **Completion:** 2005. **Gross floor area:** 4,740 m², 860 m², 626 m². **Number of workplaces:** 30, 15, 8. **Main construction:** steel framework. **Roof:** flat. **Lighting:** through façade. **Main materials:** glass, steel, wood, epoxy, plastics. **Setting:** urban.

↑ | **Interior view,** Dönges part
← | **Section**
↓ | **Framework,** axonometry

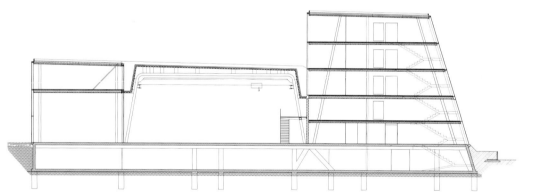

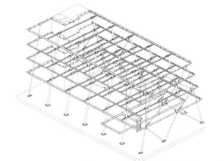

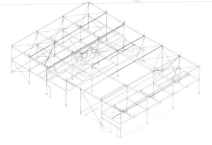

← | **Exterior view,** Wentzsche part
↓ | **Front elevation,** Wentzsche part

Archi 2000 / Philippe Verdussen

↑ | **Façade**

Tour & Taxis

Brussels

Erected at the beginning of the 20th century, the complex is designed as a concentration of maritime, rail and road networks. Designed according to rationalist theories, these buildings use steel, glass and reinforced concrete in ways that test the limits of their possibilities. Changes in customs, business and industrial practices brought about the gradual decline of the site. After many years of detrimental miscalculations, the entire site is about to be revived by the implementation of a new program utilizing a mixed approach. In an initial phase, two emblematic buildings – the Royal Warehouse and the wing – were painstakingly renovated. They are currently occupied by offices and factory premises, but they are also used for trade fairs, exhibitions and cultural events.

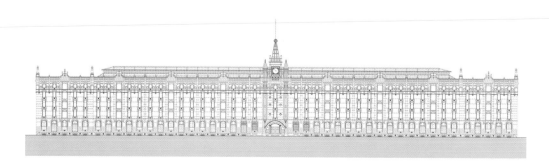

PROJECT FACTS

Address: Avenue du Port, 1000 Brussels, Belgium. **Client:** SA Tour & Taxis. **Completion:** 2005. **Gross floor area:** 60,000 m². **Number of workplaces:** 1,250. **Main construction:** steel, glass, reinforced concrete. **Roof:** glass. **Lighting:** artificial lighting and natural lighting (glass roof). **Main materials:** steel, glass. **Setting:** industrial.

↑ | **Interior**
↙ | **Elevation**

↑ | **Roof**, detail
↓ | **Exterior view**

↑ | Perspective
↗ | Front elevation
→ | Courtyard

Georg Knorr Industrial Park
Berlin

The decrepit industrial complex was renovated true to its details in the course of a close exchange with the Monument Administration. The main and side wings, the large production halls and the external complexes were transformed into a modern park, which will in part continue to be used by the Knorr company. The measures included reinforcement of the frame, roof repairs, renovation of the technical infrastructure and the reconstruction of the façades. Damaged cladding bricks and battered cut stones around doors were replaced and windows were renovated while keeping their filigree profiling. The entry hall was reconstructed using original plans. This way, a future-oriented, economical place of business could be developed through careful treatment of the historical heritage.

PROJECT FACTS Address: Georg-Knorr-Straße 4, 12681 Berlin, Germany. **Original building:** Alfred Speer. **Client:** Knorr Bremse AG. **Completion:** 2002. **Gross floor area:** 48,500 m². **Number of workplaces:** 300. **Roof:** shed. **Lighting:** through roof and façade. **Main materials:** red bricks. **Setting:** industrial.

↑ | Entrance hall
↙ | First floor plan

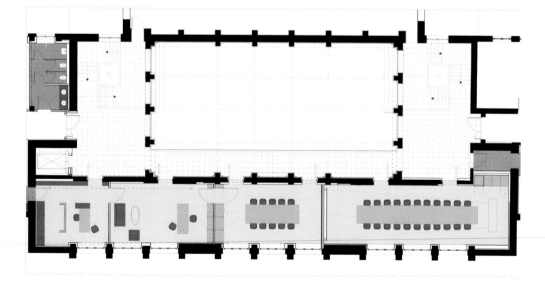

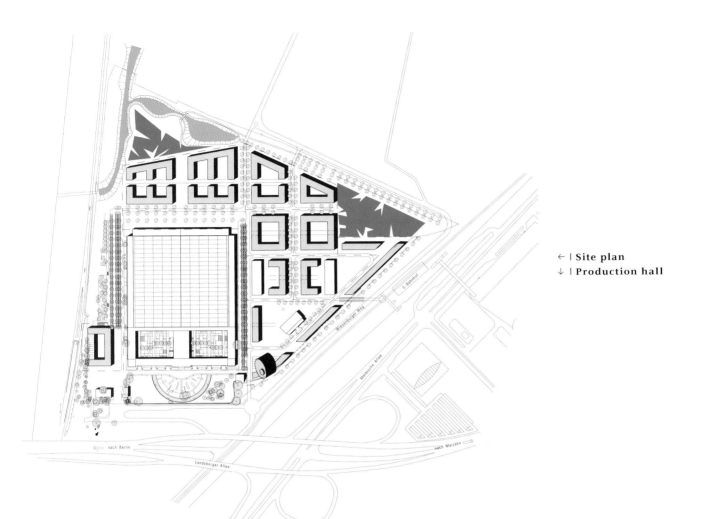

← | Site plan
↓ | Production hall

knabe & knabe
architekten+ingenieure

↑ | **Detail,** west façade

Former Porcelain Factory
Stadtlengsfeld

The conversion of the building and its premises began with the redesign of the shed hall built in 1969–1972. Starting in 1997, the 16,000 square meters were expanded and divided into independent, economical units with separate buildings for administration and management. The conversion corrected the structure's functional and climactic deficiencies using a new suspended aluminum façade which keeps moisture away from the stone structure behind it. The social and administration building is the newest structure. The volume's stories were staggered and given a projecting sun protection in order to create more shadow. Plenty of natural light and comfort-infused space is found inside, while on the exterior serves as the ensemble's opener.

PROJECT FACTS

Address: Am Fräuleinsgraben, 36457 Stadtlengsfeld, Germany. **Client:** Landesentwicklungsgesell-schaft Thüringen mbH. **Completion:** 2008. **Gross floor area:** 16,000 m². **Number of workplaces:** 130. **Main construction:** steel trussed girder on stanchions. **Roof:** shed roof, flat. **Lighting:** artificial, shed rooflight, rooflight dome. **Main materials:** aluminum-corrugated sheet metal, white plastering, glass bricks, granite floor, exposed brickwork. **Setting:** industrial.

↑ | **West façade,** color gradient
↙ | **Panorama view**

↑ | **Front façade**
↓ | **East façade**

↑ | **South-east elevation,** front façade
← | **Site plan**

← | **Interior view,** shed lights
↓ | **Interior view**

↑ | **Exterior view**
↗ | **Bird's-eye view**
→ | **Detail façade,** crash-barriers
→→ | **Detail façade** glass panneling

Business Circuit

Nieuw Vennep Zuid

Business Circuit, a multi-tenant building for small businesses, actually consists of two separate units. In order to create visual and functional unity, a coherent, striking exterior was chosen for both buildings. Crash-barriers, easily recognizable along the Dutch motorways, have been used as façade material. The rough texture of this material enhances the buildings' strong industrial appearance, whereas glass paneling in the façade has been detailed with great care. The linear graphics appearing on the surrounding road surface are a reference to the crash-barriers used in the façade. This makes the name "Business Circuit" easily spring to mind.

PROJECT FACTS

Address: Lireweg 12–80, Nieuw Vennep Zuid, The Netherlands. **Client:** Meerschip B.V. **Completion:** 2002. **Gross floor area:** 6,000 m². **Main construction:** steel framework. **Roof:** flat. **Lighting:** through façade. **Main materials:** crash-barriers and glass. **Setting:** industrial.

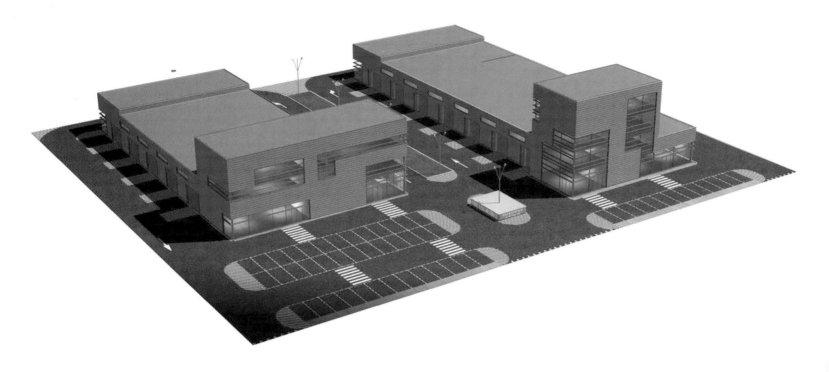

itects Index

4a architekti

Na Valech 2
16000 Prague (Czech Republic)
T +420.2.33350720
F +420.2.33355696
mail@architekti4a.cz
www.architekti4a.cz

agiplan integrale bauplanung GmbH – Architektur Generalplanung Projektmanagement

Philosophenweg 31–33
47051 Duisburg (Germany)
T +49.203.94040
F +49.203.9404180
info@aibonline.de
www.aibonline.de

Aigner-Architecture

Grafinger Straße 6
81671 Munich (Germany)
T +49.89.18908890
F +49.89.189088999
ma@aigner-architecture.com
www.aigner-architecture.com

Amann Architekten BDA

Archi 2000

Avenue du Vivier d'Oie 4 / Diesdellelaan 4
1000 Brussels (Belgium)
T +32.2.3758720
F +32.2.375756800
www.archi2000.be
info@archi2000.be

Architekten.3P Feuerstein Rüdenauer & Partner

Industriestraße 25
70565 Stuttgart (Germany)
T +49.711.78284889
F +49.711.78284891
g.feuerstein@architekten3p.de
www.architekten3p.de

Arkitema

Frederiksgade 32
8000 Aarhus C (Denmark)
T +45.70117011
F +45.86137011
arh@arkitema.dk
www.arkitema.com

Ryuichi Ashizawa Architects & associates

Nakajima-BLD.3F, 1-1-4 Nakazaki-nishi, Kita-ku
Osaka 530-0015 (Japan)
T +81.6.64852017
F +81.6.64852033
a-i@r-a-architects.com
www.r-a-architects.com

ATP Architects and Engineers

Heiliggeiststraße 16
6010 Innsbruck (Austria)
T +43.512.53700
F +43.512.53701100
info@atp.ag
www.atp.ag

b&k+ brandlhuber & co

Schöneberger Ufer 65
10785 Berlin (Germany)
T +49.171.8676084
mail@brandlhuber.com
www.brandlhuber.com

Banz + Riecks Dipl. Ing. Architekten BDA

Friederikastraße 86
44795 Bochum (Germany)
T +49.234.34190
F +49.234.34260
info@banz-riecks.de
www.banz-riecks.de

→ **142**

Barkow Leibinger Architekten

Schillerstraße 94
10625 Berlin (Germany)
T +49.30.3157120
F +49.30.31571229
info@barkowleibinger.com
www.barkowleibinger.com

→ **132**

Architektur Hansulrich Benz

Ölmühle 3
71287 Weissach (Germany)
T +49.7152.330011
F +49.7152.3300123
architektur@HansulrichBenz.de
www.HansulrichBenz.de

→ **210**

Patrick Berger et Jacques Anziutti Architectes

91, rue Réaumur
75002 Paris (France)
T +33.1.40130868
F +33.1.40139660
secretariat@berger-anziutti.com
www.patrickberger.fr

→ **182**

Cuno Brullmann Jean-Luc Crochon + Associés

13, rue Gracieuse
75005 Paris (France)
T +33.1.55433131
F +33.1.55433132
office@brullmann-crochon.com
www.brullmann-crochon.com

→ **196**

BVN Architecture – Bligh Voller Nield

PO Box N646, Grosvenor Place
NSW 1220 Sydney (Australia)
T +61.2.82977200
F +61.2.82977299
sydney@bvn.com.au
www.bvn.com.au

→ **174**

crossboundaries architects

Dongsi Dhisitiao, # 93, Bldg. A, 4th floor
Beijing 10007 (China)
T +86.10.64012553
info@crossboundaries.net
www.crossboundaries.net

→ **178**

Despang Architekten

Am Graswege 5
30169 Hanover (Germany)
T +49.511.882840
F +49.511.887985
info@despangarchitekten.de
www.despangarchitekten.de

→ **84**

Ehrlich Architects

10865 Washington Boulevard
Culver City, CA 90232 (USA)
T +1.310.8389700
F +1.310.8389737
info@ehrlicharchitects.com
www.ehrlicharchitects.com

→ **230**

Endo Shuhei Architect Institute

2-14-5 Tenma, Kita-ku
Osaka-city 530-0043 (Japan)
T +81.6.63547456
F +81.6.63547457
endo@paramodern.com
www.paramodern.com

→ **202**

FOBA

34-3 Tanaka Todo
Uji-city 611-0013 (Japan)
T +81.774.200787
F +81.774.209888
info@fob-web.co.jp
www.fob-web.co.jp

→ **206**

Foster + Partners

Riverside 22 Hester Road
London SW11 4AN (United Kingdom)
T +44.22.77380455
F +44.22.77381107
enquiries@fosterandpartners.com
www.fosterandpartners.com

Architekturbüro Früh

Lochbachstraße 6
6971 Hard (Austria)
T +43.5574.77447
F +43.5574.7744710
frueh@frueh.at
www.frueh.at

A. Furrer und Partner AG

Lorrainestrasse 15b
3013 Berne (Switzerland)
T +41.31.3306100
F +41.31.3306101
mail@furrer-partner.ch
www.furrer-partner.ch

GATERMANN + SCHOSSIG
Architekten Generalplaner

Richartzstraße 10
50667 Cologne (Germany)
T +49.221.9258210
F +49.221.92582170
info@gatermann-schossig.de
www.gatermann-schossig.de

Manuelle Gautrand Architecture

36, boulevard de la Bastille
75012 Paris (France)
T +33.1.56950646
F +33.1.56950647
contact@manuelle-gautrand.com
www.manuelle-gautrand.com

Gerken Architekten+Ingenieure

Hahnengasse 21
89073 Ulm (Germany)
T +49.731.1538920
F +49.731.15389220
info@gerken-architekten.de
www.gerken-architekten.de

GROUP A

Pelgrimsstraat 3
3029 BH Rotterdam (The Netherlands)
T +31.10.2440193
F +31.10.2449990
mail@groupa.nl
www.groupa.nl

Guedes+DeCampos

Rua São Francisco, 5, 3º
4050-548 Porto (Portugal)
T +351.222.010451
F +351.222.010451
info@guedesdecampos.com
www.guedesdecampos.com

Melkan Gursel & Murat Tabanlioglu

Mesrutiyet Cad. No. 67 Beyoglu
34430 Istanbul (Turkey)
T +90.212.2512111
F +90.212.2512332
info@tabanlioglu.com.tr
www.tabanlioglu.com.tr

Bob Gysin + Partner BGP Architekten ETH SIA BSA

Ausstellungsstrasse 24, Postfach
8021 Zurich (Switzerland)
T +41.44.2784040
F +41.44.2784050
info@bgp.ch
www.bgp.ch

Henn Architekten

Augustenstraße 54
80333 Munich (Germany)
T +49.89.523570
F +49.89.52357123
info@henn.com
www.henn.com

→ 18

IPRO DRESDEN Planungs- und Ingenieuraktiengesellschaft

Schnorrstraße 70
01069 Dresden (Germany)
T +49.351.4651728
F +49.351.4651701
ipro@ipro-dresden.de
www.ipro-dresden.de

→ 154

J.S.K Dipl. Ing. Architekten

Hainer Weg 50
60599 Frankfurt/Main (Germany)
T +49.69.60910954
F +49.69.60910980
jsk-frankfurt@jsk.de
www.jsk.de

→ 244

kab Architekten GmbH

Erich-Herion-Straße 27
70736 Fellbach (Germany)
T +49.711.5856646
F +49.711.58566470
info@kab-online.de
www.kab-architekten.de

→ 72, 204

Khanna Schultz

325 Sackett Street
Brooklyn, NY 11231 (USA)
T +1.718.2225071
F +1.718.2225073
info@khannaschultz.com
www.khannaschultz.com

→ 220, 224, 226

knabe&knabe architekten+ingenieure

Am Bahnhof 12
98529 Suhl (Germany)
T +49.3681.79930
F +49.3681.799320
kk.architektur@t-online.de

→ 248

APA Kurylowicz & Associates

Berezyńska 25
03-908 Warsaw (Poland)
T +48.22.6163798
F +48.22.6163799
apaka@apaka.com.pl
www.apaka.com.pl

→ 146

Laatio Architects Ltd.

Isokatu 19 B
90100 Oulu (Finland)
T +358.10.2309300
F +358.10.2309301
first.last@laatioark.fi
www.laatioark.fi

→ 52

Lapointe Architects

606-10 Saint Mary Street
Toronto, ON M4Y 1P9 (Canada)
T +1.416.9646641
F +1.416.9646643
francis@lapointe-arch.com
www.lapointe-arch.com

→ 214

Søren Robert Lund Architects

Store Kongensgade 110E, 1.sal
1264K Copenhagen (Denmark)
T +45.33910100
F +45.33914510
srl@srlarkitekter.dk
www.srlarkitekter.dk

→ 30

N Maeda Atelier

Glass House 1F, 1-9-5 Izumi-Honcho, Komae-shi
Tokyo 201-0003 (Japan)
T +81.3.34800064
F +81.3.54388363
norisada@sepia.ocn.ne.jp
www5a.biglobe.ne.jp/~norisada

→ 36

MDN Marco Visconti & Partners, Maire Engineering

Lungo Po Cadorna 7
10124 Turin (Italy)
T +39.011.19715601
F +39.011.19715072
info@mdnpartners.it
www.mdnpartners.it

→ 48, 86

Meyer Shircore and associates architects

PO BOX 1294
Subiaco, WA 6904 (Australia)
T +61.8.93818511
F +61.8.93881339
msa@meyershircore.com.au
www.meyershircore.com.au

→ 46

Arkitektfirmaet C. F. Møller

Europaplads 2, 11
8000 Aarhus C (Denmark)
T +45.87305300
F +45.87305399
cfmoller@cfmoller.com
www.cfmoller.com

→ 64

Nägeliarchitekten

Lychener Straße 43
10435 Berlin (Germany)
T +49.30.61609712
F +49.30.61609714
buero@naegeliarchitekten.de
www.naegeliarchitekten.de

→ 134

Nikken Sekkei Ltd.

2-18-3 Iidabashi, Chiyoda-ku
Tokyo 102-8117 (Japan)
T +81.3.52263030
F +81.3.52263044
webmaster@nikken.co.jp
www.nikken.co.jp

→ 122

O.F.D.A. associates

14 Araki-tyo, Shinjuku-ku
Tokyo (Japan)
T +81.3.33584303
F +81.3.33584304
sakaushi@ofda.jp
www.ofda.jp

→ 234

Dominique Perrault Architecture

6, rue Bouvier
75011 Paris (France)
T +33.1.440600
F +33.1.44060001
dpa@d-p-a.fr
www.perraultarchitecte.com

→ 82

pfeifer. kuhn. architekten

Gartenstraße 19
79098 Freiburg (Germany)
T +49.761.2967690
F +49.761.29676920
architekten@pfeifer-kuhn.de
www.pfeifer-kuhn.de

→ 118

project A.01 architects

Mariahilfer Straße 101/2/27
1060 Vienna (Austria)
T +43.1.5268826
F +43.1.5269991
office@projecta01.com
www.projecta01.com

→ 114

DI Rolf Rauner architektur+werkstätte

Alberstraße 8/17
8010 Graz (Austria)
T +43.650.2500498
rolf.rauner@architektur-rauner.at
www.architektur-rauner.at

→ 160

Prof. J. Reichardt Architekten BDA

Im Walpurgistal 10
45136 Essen (Germany)
T +49.201.269472
F +49.201.269475
home@reichardt-architekten.de
www.reichardt-architekten.de

→ 22, 34

RGA Arquitectes

carrer Muntaner 320 1r 1a
08021 Barcelona (Spain)
T +34.93.4141954
F +34.93.4143205
rga@rga.es
www.rga.es

→ 100

Rojkind Arquitectos

Campor Eliseos 432, Col. Polanco
Mexico-City, 11560 (Mexico)
T +49.52.55.52808521
F +49.52.55.52808396
info@rojkindarquitectos.com
www.rojkindarquitectos.com

→ 188

Philippe Samyn and Partners architects & engineers

Chaussée de Waterloo 1537
1180 Brussels (Belgium)
T +32.2.3749060
F +32.2.3747550
sai@samynandpartners
www.samynandpartners

→ 170

sarl Sandrolini Architecte

15, boulevard de Bercy
75012 Paris (France)
T +33.1.43469135
F +33.1.43415913
sandroarchi@wanadoo.fr
www.sandrolini-architecte.fr

→ 192

seifert.stoeckmann@formalhaut

Mörfelder Landstraße 72
60598 Frankfurt/Main (Germany)
T +49.69.61991552
F +49.69.61991545
seifert.stoeckmann@formalhaut.de
www.formalhaut.de

→ 150

tecARCHITECTURE Swiss AG

Lankenbergstrasse 14
8272 Ermatingen (Switzerland)
T +41.71.2290000
F +41.71.2290011
mknorr@tecarchitecture.com
www.tecarchitecture.com

→ 138

tecDESIGN studio

5455 Wilshire Blvd., Suite 2200
Los Angeles, CA 90012 (USA)
T +1.323.9338000
F +1.323.9388900
sknorr@tecarchitecture.com
www.tecarchitecture.com

→ 138

Bernard Tschumi Architects

227 West 17th Street
New York, NY 10011 (USA)
T +1.212.8076340
F +1.212.2423693
nyc@tschumi.com
www.tschumi.com

→ 164

Valode et Pistre architectes

115, rue du Bac
75007 Paris (France)
T +33.1.53632200
F +33.1.53632209
info@v-p.com
www.valode-et-pistre.com

→ 108

Michael Wilford

Lone Oak Hall, Chuck Hatch
Headfield, TN7 4EX (United Kingdom)
T +44.1892.770980
F +44.1892.770040
office@michaelwilford.com
www.michaelwilford.com

→ 134

COLLECTION OF...

Michelle Galindo
Collection: European Architecture
English | German | French
Hardcover with dust jacket
25 x 29 cm, 9 ³/₄ x 11 ¹/₂ in.
512 pages
1400 illustrations
ISBN 978-3-03768-011-7
€ 68.00 (D) | £ 49.95 | $ 89.95

Michelle Galindo
Collection: Houses
English | German | French
Hardcover with dust jacket
25 x 29 cm, 9 ³/₄ x 11 ¹/₂ in.
512 pages
1400 illustrations
ISBN 978-3-03768-012-4
€ 68.00 (D) | £ 49.95 | $ 89.95

sample pages Collection Houses

www.braun-publishing.ch

IMPRINT

The Deutsche Bibliothek is registering this publication in the Deutsche Nationalbibliographie; detailed bibliographical information can be found on the Internet at http://dnb.ddb.de

ISBN 978-3-03768-005-6

© 2009 by Braun Publishing AG
www.braun-publishing.ch

1st edition 2009

Editorial staff: Nicolai Beck, Marek Heinel, Natascha Saupe
Translation: Alice Bayandin
Graphic concept: ON Grafik | Tom Wibberenz
Layout: Marek Heinel, Natascha Saupe, Georgia van Uffelen
Reproduction: Bild1Druck GmbH, Berlin